Where Time Stood Still

by
The Reverend Watkins Leigh Ribble, D.D.

1902–1979

Retired Archdeacon of the
Episcopal Diocese of Virginia

iUniverse, Inc.
New York   Bloomington

Where Time Stood Still

iUniverse books may be ordered through booksellers or by contacting:

iUniverse
1663 Liberty Drive
Bloomington, IN 47403
www.iuniverse.com
1-800-Authors (1-800-288-4677)

Because of the dynamic nature of the Internet, any Web addresses or links contained in this book may have changed since publication and may no longer be valid.

ISBN: 978-1-4502-2425-3 (sc)
ISBN: 978-1-4502-2426-0 (ebk)

Library of Congress Control Number: 2010905199

Printed in the United States of America

iUniverse rev. date: 5/10/2010

Thoughts from a Mountaineer

The year is now 2010. The book, *Where Time Stood Still*, was privately published some thirty years ago, and copies were preserved within the family. More recently, Reverend Ribble's niece, Virginia Leigh Ribble MacKay-Smith, wondered if the book would be of interest to me, given my mountaineer background and my interest in publishing, and she reluctantly gave up one of her last copies for my comments.

I grew up in the Blue Ridge in the 1930–40s from ancestry that had migrated there in the late 1700s, early 1800s. While we were not quite the stoic crowd the Central Blue Ridge folks were, there were many similarities, such as the clannishness of families, the reaching out to a neighbor, the desire to take care of any problems within the family or the mountains, and the focus on the church as the center of their life and social world.

As a writer and one who loves the beauty of the past and the Blue Ridge Mountains, it was obvious to me that Reverend Ribble's book needed to be published in a modern vehicle. With some encouragement, this is now being done by his children, Margaret Ribble Caruthers, Pattie Ribble Chappell and W. Leigh Ribble, Jr.

The book is recommended to those interested in the past, particularly the Blue Ridge Mountains, and to those who just enjoy good reading.

Mark W. Royston,
Author of *Too Poor to Paint, Too Proud to Whitewash*;
The Spout Spring;
The Wildcat Den; and
The Faces Behind the Bases.

Photo Enhancement by Sarah Apke

Forward

The Reverend Watkins Leigh Ribble, D. D., the author of these delightful stories about the Blue Ridge Mountain people, was born in Santa Maria da Bocca do Monte, Rio Grande do Sul, Brazil, in 1902. He was the first child of an Episcopal priest who was at that time a missionary in Brazil. When Leigh was around three years old, he returned to the United States with his parents and his baby sister Mary. Leigh attended the Episcopal High School in Alexandria, Virginia, then the University of Virginia in Charlottesville, Virginia, graduating with a Bachelor of Arts Degree and a Phi Beta Kappa key. He then attended the Protestant Episcopal Theological Seminary in Alexandria, Virginia, and was ordained an Episcopal priest upon his graduation from the Seminary in 1927.

During the summer months while attending the Seminary, he worked in the mission field of the Blue Ridge Mountains, where he met his wife, Constance, whom he described in the chapter entitled "Run! Call the Mission Lady."

Leigh and Constance were married after his graduation from the Seminary and returned to Brazil as missionaries. Unfortunately, they had to return to the United States after two years because Leigh had contracted tuberculosis. After he recovered his health, he returned to Stanardsville, Virginia, where he served as priest in charge of seven missions from 1930 to 1935. He then became Rector of The Falls Church, which was established in the early 1700s in Falls Church, Virginia. In 1945 he became Rector of Grace and Holy Trinity Church in Richmond, Virginia, and served there until 1962 when he became Archdeacon of the Episcopal Diocese of Virginia. He retired in 1968 and died on September 19, 1979.

Leigh had many hobbies. For example, he was an avid gardener throughout his life, raising both vegetables and flowers; he grew beautiful orchids in his greenhouse. He was an amateur magician and enjoyed using his magic to entertain patients in the hospital. He raised bees. He was a very good chess player. He was a golfer. He was a voracious reader and scholar. He was a humorist and a gifted storyteller.

He had a deep interest in the Civil War. He visited many of the Civil War battlefields. He owned a complete set of the official records of that war, many of which he had read and studied. As the Bishop of Virginia wrote at the time of Leigh's death, "We used to take trips together to visit the missions. I learned a great deal about Civil War history. When we went to an historic site, you felt that he'd actually been there. He had an extraordinary memory."

Leigh also had a strong interest in people. He was a member of and Chaplain for the Society of the Cincinnati in Virginia as well as a member of many other organizations, both social and historical.

Among many resolutions passed at the time of his death, the Vestry of Grace and Holy Trinity passed the following:

"VESTRY RESOLUTION HONORS FORMER RECTOR
WATKINS LEIGH RIBBLE

"WHEREAS, Watkins Leigh Ribble, D.D., served this church as rector for seventeen years, bringing to bear his considerable gift of intellect and pastoral care; and

"WHEREAS, he sought to base his whole manner of life and ministry on the sure foundation of the Gospel, and Gospel alone; and

"WHEREAS, he constantly reminded his people of their need to witness and minister to the whole world beyond their doorstep, lifting their vision and challenging their effort; and

"WHEREAS, he graced and enlivened many an occasion with his wit and charm, bringing good humor, enthusiasm and zest; and

"WHEREAS, he exhibited a faithfulness and dedication that made a lasting impact on many lives; now

"THEREFORE MAY IT BE RESOLVED, that the Clergy/Vestry, and wider congregation of Grace and Holy Trinity Church record their thanksgiving for the ministry of Watkins Leigh Ribble, both here and elsewhere."

Contents

Preface

My close association with the people of the Blue Ridge Mountains covered nearly a generation between the years 1921 and 1940 and was geographically confined chiefly to the Virginia counties of Greene, Albemarle, Madison, Page and Buckingham. When I first came to know the mountain folk, they were beginning to awaken from what appeared to be a long sleep. They were yet living, thinking and working as their forefathers did for centuries and were still clinging stubbornly to the ancient customs of their culture. Ere long vast changes would sweep this primitive civilization away and the picturesque mountaineer of story and legend would become a fading memory. However, I saw few signs of this at the time and felt in truth the foreigner they took me to be.

Life among them during this period provided a variety of experiences, ranging from the tragic to the comic. Over the years since then, friends who listened kindly to my account of them insisted, "Why don't you write these things up? Those days are gone now. People are forgetting what they were like. If anyone does not record them, they will be lost." In time, the tempter whispered more and more persistently, "Why not?" So here is the result, culled from copious notes set down at the time they happened and from a memory in which little has grown dim.

There is no intention of offering a consecutive narrative, but to present a series of stories, each complete in itself, but all merging into a larger picture of a place, time and people as one person saw it.

Family names and the names of individuals for the most part are authentic, but some have been changed for the sake of the person still living. Also, now and then, places have been made vague in order to obviate embarrassment. Except for these three conversational pieces – Roadside Chat, Feed Store Theology, and Minding the Store – events happened substantially as described, but I cannot vouch for the genuineness of "hearsay" items. The conversation pieces are edited compilations of actual chit-chats listened to on many occasions. They are offered to provide insights and local color which could not be inserted elsewhere in the narrative.

An effort has been made to keep dialect to a plausible minimum. The Virginia Blue Ridge mountaineer had and still has to some extent a special mode of speech but it has been grossly exaggerated in reporting, even to the point of ridicule.

Dialect is most difficult to put on paper and can get so out of hand that it becomes well-nigh unreadable. Much depends on the ear of the writer. If two persons listen to the same mountain conversation and separately write it out, even assisted by notes, the difference between the two would be striking, because different people do not hear unfamiliar speech sounds the same way.

Then too, mountain people speak differently in different places, and even in the same place. Not all drop the final –ings; nor do all, for example, say kotch for catch; keer for care; kin for can; git for get. Double negatives are common but not universal, and a- before a present participle is less than common. To generalize: the speech of the woman tends to have more variants than that of their men who have more contact with the outside world; the more isolated the people, the more archaisms sprinkle their conversations which show marked differences in pronunciation and vocabulary; the more education they have, the less distinctive their language.

My hope is that in these pages the mountain folk have been treated with sympathy, as well as candor, for such is my aim. When one has lived through certain events and experiences, he is never sure how fair he is in reporting them. If offense is given to friends by chance, it was done unwittingly. For many in the Blue Ridge Mountains are and have been close friends, to whom I owe a great deal of affection and gratitude.

W. Leigh Ribble

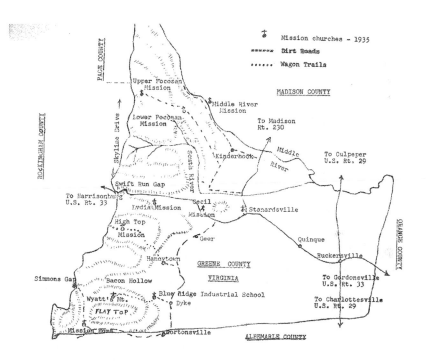

1922--WLR (Watkins Leigh Ribble), a student at the University of Virginia. He graduated with a BA degree in 1924.

1924—Constance Murray Strobel (CMS) and Margaret Lawrence at the Blue Ridge Industrial School. CMS was a young mountain mission worker. She married WLR in 1927. Margaret Lawrence was a mountain mission worker and nurse. (See Chapter 2)

1924—Same as photo 2.

1924—WLR in Greene County on the way to Haneytown.

1925—CMS with Mrs. Puss Shifflet on Wyatt's Mountain, Greene Co.

1927—WLR in Covesville, Va., recently graduated from The Virginia Theological Seminary, in Alexandria, VA.

1927—WLR and CMR (two center figures in photo) arrive in Rio de Janeiro. CMS married WLR in 1927. WLR was a missionary in Brazil from 1927 to 1929. However, he and his family were forced to leave Brazil in 1929, after he was stricken with tuberculosis. They returned to Virginia, where WLR spent several months in a sanitarium.

1930— In Stanardsville, WLR holds his first child, daughter Margaret, born in 1929 in Brazil.

1932—In Stanardsville, WLR with daughter Margaret. They are surrounded by their pigeons, which they raise for food.

1932—In Stanardsville, parents of WLR hold their granddaughter Margaret. The grandparents are Rev. George W. Ribble, D.D. and Pattie Ribble. Like his son WLR, G. W. Ribble had been a missionary in Brazil when he was a young man.

1933—In Stanardsville, WLR works in his garden, which was an important source of food for his family.

1934—In Stanardsville, WLR's young daughters Margaret and Pattie. In late 1934, a third child was born—son WLR Jr. In 1935, the family left Stanardsville and moved to Falls Church, Va.

Unidentified individuals

Chapter 1

WE AINT NEVER DONE NO DIFFERENT

The first time I went into the Blue Ridge Mountains to take up residence and work, I felt I had stepped back a century and a half in time. It seemed to be a Never Never Land where little had changed for a hundred and fifty years and which both civilization and history had by-passed. The glacier like movement of population from the eastern seaboard westward had spread over the Appalachia and moved on, leaving behind in the valleys, coves , and hollows, ground moraines of people, who had no significant part in the commercial, industrial, and cultural development of the country. The rugged terrain, the absence of good roads, the lack of skills for developing the slender resources of a difficult environment, and the dearth of creative contacts with the outside world, locked them into enclaves where they long remained virtually undisturbed. They were severed from the dynamic life of a growing nation of which they knew less and less, and feared more and more. So little were they a part of it that they regarded themselves as surrounded by foreigners and felt safe only in their isolation.

Time slowed to a stop. Change was resisted. Each year became more like the last, and, even though their hard lives developed the strong virtues of independence and self-reliance, dreary sameness numbed the spirit. So they clung to the old ways of speech and to the customs of dead generations in which they found a measure of stability, "'Cause this is the way it always was."

Once the first shock had worn off, it was not too difficult to get used to their dialect. One's ear readily got accustomed to it, and in the hills it sounded very natural indeed. With time, it ceased to be a quaint experience when I encountered a mountaineer walking along a road who was glad to stop for a chat and learned that he felt "tol'able peart" and that his wife and children "were well as common"; that he was hurrying home from the crossroads store where he had bought some "vittles" which he was carrying in his "poke"; that he didn't have time to tarry long "'cause home's a right fur piece and the old woman's looking for me to git thar soon with the fixings so's she can cook up a mess for me and the family"; that he was " proud to meet up with me" and hoped that "we'll meet again soon, if I live."

Getting used to their way of doing things posed the greater problem, and I could never become adjusted to some practices that had the status and acceptance of custom. The latter clustered mainly around the position of women in the mountain home and society. Not to be forgotten was the first sight of a husband riding on his horse up a steep grade and his wife walking along behind them burdened with a sack of vegetables. No matter how many times I saw similar scenes, they never failed to cause feelings of anger and in this respect I was always a "foreigner". Sometimes the wife carried a baby as she followed husband and horse. When a husband was on foot, his wife dutifully walked three paces behind him, with or without a load. No wonder mountain women used to grow old so young. Their lives were hard enough as it was without having this menial station imposed on them. Happily, little of this is seen nowadays.

The men certainly found life burdensome, scratching, as best they could, a living from a hostile soil which would seldom allow them to rise above the poverty level. However, they expected their women to "fetch and carry" for them in addition to taking care of the tasks about home and garden, not to mention working in the fields at planting and harvest time. The men worked the crops, looked after the animals, and hunted game, as far back as can be remembered, but they never touched the kitchen gardens. This was beneath their dignity. They wanted the usual vegetables to eat: 'taters, snaps, turnips, beets, onions, and cabbage, but raising them was woman's work.

Added to these indignities was the custom of men first at the table at mealtime, with the womenfolk remaining out of sight in the kitchen unless needed to render some service or to bring in more food. In the early days of my stay, being new to this I found the custom difficult to get along with. During my first meal in a mountain home, my host asked me if I wanted more bread, assuring me there was plenty more in the stove. I accepted the offer and immediately he shouted through the closed kitchen door, "Old lady! Preacher wants more biscuits!" Once the men folk were taken care of and had left the table, then it was the turn of the women and children.

This type of separation by sex extended beyond the home. In public meetings and especially at church services, chairs, benches, or pews were arranged in two sections divided by an aisle. The men sat on the right. The women and children sat on the left. The men walked in and out as they chose. The women and children stayed put except in emergencies. Growing boys looked forward to the day when they would be considered old enough to escape from the women and sit with their fathers or with their peers. This would be a big step toward dignity and freedom. Afterward, they coveted the coming of that indefinable time, when they would be allowed to declare their manhood by joining the masculine parade in and out with none to say them nay. When that time arrived had to be discovered by trial and error. The first trials were usually abortive, as an eager fledgling's first efforts usually are. A parental hiss, "Git back thar whar you belong" made it clear that childhood was not over yet. But in due time, the attempt would be unopposed. That was a proud moment, for the boy then felt he was accepted as a man.

This might be a great day for the budding youngster, but it was also the beginning of some anxiety for his parents and even for the adults in the area. Would he be a peaceable kind of fellow or would he run "hog wild?" There was cause for concern as there was so little for young people to do over weekends and also when the farming season was over. Pent up energies had not much outlet outside of physical labor which was sporadic beyond home chores. Spare time could be trouble time for youths for whom life was often unbearable with boredom. When not occupied, they tended to cluster in congenial groups of their male peers. No girls were admitted to such gatherings. They had their own groupings. Here was where a teenage boy began experiments with life under the tutelage of those older than he. In such get-togethers, he first found out what it was like to get drunk. He added extensively to the store of such meager sex knowledge as he already had. Here he tested his physical strength and courage in fights with those of his kind. Thus "pecking orders" were established. At times relief from tedium would be sought by the group "whooping and hollering up and down the road", throwing rocks at bushes, birds, lizards, chickens, hogs, fence posts and so on as fancy dictated. Sometimes when too much whiskey might be available, fights could get serious and not a few killings resulted. On the whole, there was little vandalism and when damage was done through excess of exuberance, youths were prompt to plead that they meant no harm. Acts of violence, such as killing of livestock or setting fires to buildings, were usually committed in retaliation for some injury, real or fancied, or some insult which no man who was a man could accept. Even though such acts were not condoned, the reason for them was understood and at times sympathized with. It must be admitted that the tendency toward violence was common in mountain life and a constant source of danger.

After I had been in the Blue Ridge long enough to be accepted by the people to the point of being able to exchange views and opinions freely, I ventured to question and then to criticize certain of their ways of doing things because some of them made little sense anymore and some seemed hardly civilized. It became evident very quickly that there was a limit conferred by friendship. It was made clear in the first place that no "foreigner" has any business meddling with the usages of common folk. In the second place, the stability of a mountain community would become threatened if anyone tried to change the customs and conventions that had held steady as far back as anybody could remember, no matter how archaic they had become for the country at large.

In my youthful eagerness, I felt called upon to help bring a new day of enlightenment into the hills. Noting how the little farms erode with every rain, situated as they were on steep slopes, and observing how the land declined in fertility as the same type of crops drained it of productiveness each succeeding year, I was sure I had a duty to set things right, particularly as it was evident that the great poverty of the people grew out of the condition of the soil. So I spoke enthusiastically of terracing to prevent the dirt from washing away; of contour plowing as a further guard against deadly erosion; of planting and plowing crops under to increase humus and fertility; of raising a greater variety of vegetables than they were accustomed to in order to add diversity and flavor to their diet. Mercifully I will pass over certain suggestions to change mountain partiality to fried and boiled foods, swimming in grease, which were hard to consume unless one happened to be downright ravenous.

It was made abundantly clear that in such a static society, new ideas and new methods were anathema. Not a few young people were dissatisfied with the order in which they found themselves trapped. Some escaped, but most were cowed into silence and compliance by public opinion. There was no use in arguing that the world had passed them by and that it was time to catch up. The invariable response was, "We don't hold with those people out there, noways. What we do suits us. This is the way my pa did it and it is the way his pa did it. We ain't never done no different." What leadership I was exercising then might have been lost had not the people developed a friendly tolerance toward me and said among themselves, "Don't mind him. He's a foreigner and don't understand about us yet. He'll l'arn though. He don't mean no harm."

But this state of affairs could not last. The solid front against change began to crack and crumble even before the 1930's, not everywhere nor at the same rate, to be sure. In some areas of Appalachia, it was like a dam giving way slowly and then with a rush. In others, little seems to have happened to this day. In the northern part of the Blue Ridge Mountains of Virginia, and particularly in Greene County, little of the old is left. The outside foreign world found its way in. The establishment of the Shenandoah National Park in 1935 displaced most of the mountain families when the Federal Government bought up their homes and farms. Some settled in sight of their native hills, unable to abandon their homeland. Others scattered to far places, finding a new life and a new challenge, which not only provided an escape from the old grinding hardships but also a much healthier and happier existence. A number, alas, transferred their poverty to new localities, largely in northern industrial cities, where the demand for unskilled labor was minimal, and where, unable to compete, they were worse off than before, having exchanged the hills for slums.

The breakdown of the old isolation was spurred by the development of a good road system, eliminating most of the old dirt roads which became impassable in winter. These improved, and hard surfaced roads let outsiders in and the insiders out. Automobiles proliferated from almost zero to considerable numbers within the area. Traffic swelled and business picked up markedly with the growing demand for goods and services. Power lines at first stuck closely to the main highways, but, in time, put out tendrils that curled their way along the side roads and up into the hollows and the coves. They brought not only light and power but also the incursion of the world of radio, and, of late, television. No people can be subjected to the spell of such magic and remain the same, nor stay content with poverty, no matter how dignified, as reports of the abundant life beyond their ken filtered into their homes through loud-speakers.

More and better schools made their impact. Over the years, they have heavily cut down the former high rate of illiteracy. Children, who once were the only ones in the family "with l'arning" and who used to read newspapers to and write letters for their elders, are now elders anxious for their children to get the best education for life in this changing world where a strong back alone cannot ensure a decent living. Now it is commonly agreed that education, far from ruining a good plow-hand, is the only escape they have from the destitution which has withered people in the mountains for generations.

Here and there, however, desperate efforts are still being made to throw up dikes to turn aside this flooding in of the new. Oldsters, particularly, try to hold on to the old customs which prevailed so long. But the struggle is all but lost as the young break away from the stifling past. The elders, as always, are fearful of drastic changes and ascribe them to the working of the devil and his angels. They complain as they view the wreckage of the culture they knew and still cherish, "Things ain't what they used to be. Children have gone wild and don't listen to their parents no more. What are we all coming to?"

In certain sections, a two way movement of people has developed. On the way out are the ambitious young who see no future for themselves in the Blue Ridge. They do not intend to sever their home ties and in years to come will return whenever possible for reunions and "to visit the old folks." As they go out, they are passed by a growing current of people flowing in from the cities and the suburbs looking for bargains in land around the edges of the Shenandoah National Park, which did not swallow up all the mountain territory. The best bargains have been snapped up and the price of even poor land has soared. Some mountain farmers have made what is to them fortunes by dividing their holdings into lots which have been eagerly bought by the "foreigners" regardless of quality and frequently without investigating the availability of water.

These newcomers do not intend to become permanent residents, except for a few retirees. More and more inhabitants of Suburbia and Megalopolis are discovering the Blue Ridge as a place "to get away from it all". Thither they flee temporarily from crowds, traffic, and concrete. There they find a brief respite from urban tensions and rest from noise and confusion on weekends and vacation periods. The fear of nuclear warfare touched off a search for refuge after World War II. In a panicky mood, many families felt they might have some chance for surviving a holocaust if they could get to the mountains from target cities like Washington, Baltimore, Norfolk and Richmond. This fear has faded, and in its place is the pleasure of having a quiet spot in the highlands where one can go and take it easy for a while.

Time no longer stands still in Appalachia, for the twentieth century is steadily swallowing up the remains of the eighteenth and nineteenth. The process is far from complete because many areas have changed little and others still retain vestiges of the old days. To venture a prediction: after two more generations have passed, hill-billy jokes will have become meaningless and the mountaineer will no longer be classified as a latter day barbarian and pitied for his ignorance and poverty. One of them put it this way: "The time's a-coming when we will be just like other folks."

Chapter 2

RUN! CALL THE MISSION LADY

A hush settled over the pupils of the third and fourth grade classroom of the Blue Ridge Industrial School for mountain children. Their young teacher had just made a peculiar request of them,

"Please call me in fifteen minutes. I have got to close my eyes."

Then she put her head down on the desk and fell sound asleep, even though the morning was only half gone. The children knew very well what the trouble was. They did not call her in fifteen minutes. They let her sleep for two hours while they quietly did their assigned lessons.

Two days before, at about four o'clock, the older students and the youngest member of the faculty, working in the school cannery, had almost finished putting up seemingly endless bushels of peaches for the winter. The young teacher, along with the rest, had put in a hard day's work and was looking forward to a little rest before the time came for her to go with a group of the older girls to milk the cows, when suddenly she heard a child calling her frantically,

"Miss Strobel! Miss Strobel! Please come and hurry. Little Elsie has been burned bad and Miss Margaret ain't here!"

"Miss Margaret" was the school nurse who managed the infirmary. She was away from the school on an emergency call, for the mountain community always turned to her for help when the lone, overworked doctor in all that area could not be reached. And now at this tragic moment, she was gone. So also were Elsie's parents who were picking fruit in distant orchards and had left the four year old child in the care of her brothers and sisters. For a few moments the little girl was not watched and in that time she tried to put a pan of food on an eye of the hot wood burning stove after taking off the lid. Her sleeve caught fire and before the children could extinguish the flames, her whole dress was ablaze and the front of her body was terribly burned. Two of her sisters ran for help.

Not locating the nurse, the frightened youngsters rushed to the cannery to find the young teacher who often went with Miss Margaret on her rounds. After hearing their almost hysterical account of the accident, Miss Constance Strobel dashed to the central building of the school, snatched some soft sheets, picked up two pounds of lard along with a box of baking soda. Since she had no training for such emergencies, this was the best she could think of doing. Leaving word for someone to summon the doctor as soon as possible, she rushed off with the children to their little mountain home about a mile and a half away.

There she found the rest of the children bending over little Elsie, who was lying on the only bed in the house (most of the family slept on pallets on the floor). Her clothes had been taken off along with most of her skin. Immediately, the teacher made a paste of lard and soda, spread it on small squares of cloth cut from the sheets and laid them gently over the burned areas. She had nothing to give little Elsie to ease her pain, and the child's crying and moaning were hard to bear.

Two hours later, Miss Margaret came with the bad news that the doctor was away somewhere and that there was no telling when he might come to see the child. She brought with her some linseed oil, which took the place of the lard and soda. It was a miracle that the girl survived not only the injuries but also the crude remedies. The two women stayed with little Elsie all night, watching her carefully, changing the dressings, and sponging her feverish head. Worse, the bed was lumpy and infested with bedbugs that crawled around like ants. It was a continuous battle to keep them picked off the child and off the clothes of the women.

With morning the two women returned to the school and put in a full day's work, while little Elsie's parents took care of her. At nightfall, the weary nurses took their station once more at the bedside. The child was worse and needed close attention but fatigue was taking its toll. Miss Margaret, while being the elder, had to get some relief by taking naps while sitting in a straight back chair. The only way Miss Strobel could keep awake the second night was to concentrate on counting the bedbugs as she caught them on the child and dropping them in a can containing some kerosene. Added to the fatigue was the sickening odor of the repulsive insects mixed with the filthy smells of the house.

When morning came, the two returned to their school duties. Need for sleep overpowered Miss Strobel in the classroom. The children understood and cooperated. Also, one of little Elsie's sisters was a pupil in the third grade, and this brought the calamity very close to her classmates. Fortunately, the doctor came at last and, finding that the child was not improving, rushed her to the University Hospital. There she spent many months and had many skin grafts before she came home well and bright again. She was a most fortunate little girl, for many mountain children lost their lives from accidents, from fire, and even from firearms carelessly left where children could play with them.

An experience such as this was not unusual for the mission workers. There was no telling what new demands might be made on them each new day. Emergencies were common in areas where life was hard and mere existence was a continual risk. Beyond certain fixed duties, there was nothing resembling a job description for the mission staff. They did whatever had to be done when crises arose, never questioning if any call on them was a part of their responsibility. The people depended heavily on them in time of trouble. When sickness, accident, or death struck in a family, the almost instinctive reaction was, "Run! Call the mission lady!"

A profile of the average woman worker would conform to this outline: between forty to fifty-five years old, unmarried or widowed, high school education or better, with prior experience in some field, such as church work, social service or teaching school. She volunteered for a limited time but was liable to carry on until retirement. She was deeply dedicated, had an intense sympathy for the poor and under-privileged, was very adaptable, dogged, accepted privation and sacrifice without complaint, was steady in the face of danger or crisis, ready to respond to calls for help, occasionally likely to be soft-hearted when sternness was required, a bit naïve, and was greatly loved and respected by the mountain people, who were very protective toward her.

Though there was a pattern, there was ample variety among these women. In this respect, little Elsie's two nurses represented the two extremes between which the female missionaries fell.

Miss Strobel, nineteen years old, fresh from college, was brisk and brash. The world was hers for the taking, and she was eager to get at it. To her the ills of mankind were indeed grievous, but youth and courage would put an end to such a sorry state, once the elders parted ranks widely enough to let the coming generation through to enter the fray. Few were the questions to which she did not have an answer. Her zeal brought to mind the words of Dorothy Parker describing her youth.

"My plume on high, my flag unfurled,
I rode away to right the world.
'Come out you dogs and fight!' said I
And wept there was but once to die."

Feeling that she was held in low esteem because of her age, she was determined to show that she could acquit herself as well as any of her associates. To the uneasiness of her superiors, she had no fear of saddling up Charlie, one of the School's horses, and riding alone at will over Wyatt's Mountain, or of walking three miles by rough paths and climbing many fences to visit the families belonging to the little chapel in Haneytown. Dangers were there, but she treated them as though they did not exist, suffering no worse calamity then trying to eat a scrambled rotten egg with an expressionless face in order not to embarrass her mountain hostess, or being bitten severely by a green-eyed hound, which sneaked up behind her at Bacon Hollow. Her naivety and her spunk gave her a protective shield that carried her through many an awkward situation and kept unwanted attention at a distance. Her advent was not unnoticed by the local gallants, but such interest soon wilted as at Haneytown on her second trip there to teach Sunday School. Two swains dressed in their Sunday best appeared at the chapel, wearing straw hats with freshly picked daisies stuck in their hat bands, and sat on the front pew, smiling engagingly at the teacher. The signals were ignored and dreams withered along with the daisies. The eagerness and efficiency of this volunteer caused her to be overloaded with work, but she did not feel imposed upon, thinking that it was all part of what she had come to the mountains to do.

Miss Margaret Lawrence was nearly sixty years old, slight of build, sparrow like in her movements and gestures. She was Victorian to the core. Her clothes were practical and severe, her skirts ankle-length, and her costume was completed by a choker collar, stiffened with whalebone, which she always wore. Her dark, close fitting hat was as prim as she. Walking, sitting, or riding horseback, her posture was stiffly erect and her bearing regal. She was always dressed as though she were going to tea, even when she was answering a distress summons to Scrougeabout Hollow. She never lost her composure, nor raised her voice, no matter what the provocation. In her dealings with people, lowlander or mountaineer, she was firm, fair and gentle.

As a nurse, Miss Lawrence was largely self-taught. A desperate need existed for nursing care and, in such far-off, inaccessible places, hope for getting properly trained persons was nil at the time she came to work at the Blue Ridge Industrial School. Necessity and an aptitude for taking care of the sick spurred her into taking a correspondence course in nursing and soon after completing it, she was in great demand. Miss Lawrence rapidly became a familiar and beloved figure as she rode her horse, Teddy, side-saddle along the mountain trails on her errands. She treated snake bites, bound up cuts and wounds, sat days and nights by sick beds, and calmed panicky relatives. When the doctor was not available, which was often, she delivered many babies, as attested by the fact that not a few little girls were baptized "Margaret." The health of over a hundred boarding students of the School was in her hands each session. Under her imperious rule in the dormitories and in the infirmary, the incidence of sickness and disease was held to a minimum among the members of the student body and faculty.

It took members of a hardy breed to venture out and to stay in the hills. Misfits were soon weeded out by loneliness and harsh working conditions. But those who stayed and entered into the life of the mountain people had the satisfaction of seeing their efforts make many changes in the life style of their localities particularly in the matter of home cleanliness and hygiene, domestic furnishings and decoration, infant care, tending the sick and injured, establishing schools where needed, and in the reduction of crime and violence. The power of their influence cannot be exaggerated.

Much had to be accomplished indirectly. The pride of the mountain folk, male and female, was such that bald criticism of their ways and customs would alienate them and so would gratuitous advice about hearth and home which they would regard as an unwelcome intrusion into their personal affairs. It would be instructive to look at one of the typical mission stations, now extinct because the Shenandoah National Park took over most of the land and scattered the people.

The station consisted of a two story workers' house with a commodious living room useful for many purposes, a chapel that doubled as a school, a clothing bureau, and a couple of outbuildings. Woods surrounded the property except where the public road ran. A copious spring supplied ample water which was pumped into the residence by a ram. Large stones littered the upper part of the yard and were used as seats by the people as they sat and chatted and also as pews when very hot weather forced the congregation out of the little school-chapel to the outdoor stone altar around which they would worship.

It was a good place to gather, summer and winter, for that mountain community. The mission home was a warmly hospitable place where visitors found a cordial welcome in the large common room, which the women especially looked on as a haven. There they could listen to a battery radio, a great treat in those days; use the only phone on the mountain; catch up on the local news; or just get a change from their dull routine. There they could see the cleanliness of the building, take note that chickens did not have the run of the house, observe the bright flowered curtains at the windows and the cheery pictures on the wall—all in contrast to most of their homes. On the large table in the center, there was not only suitable reading matter, but always those two fascinating and effective civilizing agents, Sears and Roebuck and Montgomery Ward catalogues, which were in constant use. These silent influences gradually moved the women to take steps, hesitant at first, to improve their little homes, making them cleaner, brighter and more comfortable with materials purchased from the mail order house.

The clothing bureau was a valuable and necessary institution for a long time. The need of the mountain people for good warm clothes was publicized through the Diocese of Virginia from the start of the mission and the response was generous, if not overwhelming, so much so that, to house the operation, a special building had to be constructed with counters, shelves, racks and stands, to display the articles for examination and selection. The women workers had the responsibility of receiving the material and picking it over to remove unsuitable matter such as shoddy garments, men's clothing more appropriate for the club than for the hills, décolleté evening gowns, dancing slippers, huge women's hats with ostrich plumes, wispy underwear, and the like. The remaining items were then sorted out as to kind, sizes and quality and then put on display. Discarded material served many purposes when it was cut up in proper sizes for making quilts, for patching, for doll's dresses and for cleaning rags. These were highly prized by the mountain women. The whole operation was done publicly so as to avoid possible accusations of favoritism on clothing bureau days.

In the beginning, a mistake was made by adopting the policy of giving the clothes away. The workers were surprised, even hurt, when the needed articles were not only refused by most of the people but refused with hostility. They were even more shocked to discover that clothing, which seemed to be accepted, was tossed into the bushes or hung on trees at distances from the mission. Discreet inquiries quickly made it clear that the mountaineers did not want charity from "foreigners" and did not want their noses rubbed in their poverty. It offended their sense of independence and dignity.

The policy was quickly reversed. Clothing bureau days became sale days, and on every piece of goods there was a price tag. The prices were give-away prices. An undershirt might be marked ten cents, a pair of shoes seventy-five cents, a good suit coat one dollar, a hat fifty cents. But no matter, paying removed the stigma and saved pride. Those who could not pay even these prices could pay in work. The men could clean up the grounds, repair fences, and cut up wood for cooking and heating. The women could do laundry, help with the clothing bureau, and clean the residence and the school-chapel. So every clothing bureau day became a very busy day and attracted goodly crowds. The proceeds from the sales were modest and were used mainly to defray some of the expenses of the mission. However, the main purpose was fulfilled, that of getting good warm clothing to the people and particularly of reducing the illness of children during the winter.

For all their courage and aggressiveness, the women workers had difficulty in preventing fights around the mission. If one actually got under way, the men present could be counted on to break it up since the combatants were usually youths between eighteen and twenty years old. When tempers heated to the flash point between two youngsters, it was well-nigh impossible to cool them off with appeals to their "better natures" or threats of arrest. Callow antagonists felt that "backing down" would compromise their manhood, and so they would be impervious to reasoning. The prospect of jail would be ignored generally, because the chance of the threat being carried out was remote indeed if a certain ritual was followed after the excitement of a fight had died down. For each offender, the procedure was to go separately to the mission a day or two later with hat in hand and say repentantly to the mission lady, "Please 'scuse me, ma'm, for the way I done the other day. I didn't aim to make no trouble but the other fellow 'vanced on me and I had to fight. Please ma'm, let me off this time."

Normally, there would be a stern lecture from the mission lady on losing one's temper, the impropriety of such behavior around churches, the bad example set for children, and the necessity of keeping the peace in public places for everybody's good. There would be a kind of absolution with a promise not to swear out a warrant if the culprit would give his word never to do such a thing again. This done with due humility, the offender could walk away without fear of being called to account before the law. Matters would then settle down, but such lenient treatment did not ensure public tranquility even if both antagonists begged pardon.

Too often, one would follow the ritual and the other would neglect or refuse to do so. The next thing the latter knew was that he would be served with a warrant for disturbing the peace on church property, which was not lightly regarded those days. This distinction between "the good and the bad boy," far from being accepted by the people, was commonly regarded as unfair. To let one off and not the other because he had not "minded his manners" smacked of favoritism among the mountaineers, who held that those involved in offenses of this sort should be treated alike—punish both or let both off. This uneven policy tended to tarnish the image of those in authority.

Experience taught that soft-heartedness sowed more trouble than it prevented. The important thing was to stay alert at gatherings to spot signs of disorder and to head it off before violence broke out. Here the women workers could count very little on the men present. They would intervene quickly after fights started, but before it, interference could be construed as meddling in other folk's affairs and embroil more people than the antagonists. Many a "gredge" got started when inept peace efforts aroused resentments involving whole families. So volunteers for such ventures were rare indeed.

Responsibility for quenching disturbances around churches rested ultimately with the minister in charge of the field, but, with several missions, he was seldom around except for services and special meetings. At these times, he was peace officer as well as evangelist and if he was forceful and consistent, there would seldom be any difficulty. So the women workers would try to plan special programs to suit the clergyman's schedule and put heavy pressure on him to lend his presence for their peace of mind. Sometimes such tactics were amply justified.

A case in point occurred one Lent, near Good Friday, when I arranged to have a showing of some excellent slides in color illustrating the life of Jesus Christ. Out of several missions, I selected the one on Pocosan Mountain, because it was difficult for me to visit there as often as desirable on week days. Not many people were expected to be present, as the lecture had to be held after dark and few cared to go out at night. To our surprise, a large group showed up of which a considerable number were teen-agers. Behavior was excellent as I struggled with an ancient oil-lamp magic lantern. Electricity would not be available in those parts for years to come. Everything went well, and the audience seemed appreciative. After dismissing the group, my wife and I went from the chapel to the mission house, having been invited for a cup of coffee before driving back home.

Some of the mountain couples also came in for refreshments and conversation, while the younger people stayed outside to chat, since it was a rather balmy evening. All had seemed serene, but presently three girls in their teens came in all excited and pleased, eyes shining, giggling happily as they went to sit in the far corner of the common room. Soon after, two of the older women came in and whispered to the mission worker, who then went out with them. In a few minutes, she returned and called me aside.

"I don't want to upset the people in here, she said, "but there is a fight brewing out by the wood pile. You saw those girls who came in here. They are the dates of three South River boys who walked them up here tonight. Now, three boys from down toward Fletcher say that they are going to walk them home and will fight anybody who tries to stop them. I tried to reason with them, but they won't look at me, much less talk to me. Please see what you can do."

We called the girls over, and I asked them if they had done anything to provoke this situation. They shook their heads, and one of them declared that after talking with friends for a while, their party got ready to walk home, when the three Fletcher boys butt in and tried to take over. She added that the girls didn't want anything to do with those boys anyway, but all three seemed to be pleased at the fuss being made over them. So I went out and found the six swains quietly sitting on logs and trying to look unconcerned. Not a word was being said, but the air was highly charged. None of them looked at me but stared straight ahead.

My lecture was brief, telling them that I would hold them responsible for any trouble and that I would not hesitate to have them arrested if they started a fight, since I had the authority to command the peace not only on church grounds but beyond. There was no response, and the two sides stared at each other. I noticed that all the men had faded away.

There seemed to be only one solution, so I told them, "Now listen to me, I am going to break this up right now. I am not going to say who is right and who is wrong, but there is going to be no trouble. My wife and I are going to put the girls in my car and drive them down the mountain to their homes. Now you boys from down Fletcher way, leave the grounds and start up the road to where you can take the short cut to your homes. You South River boys, leave the grounds and start down the road to where you belong. I'll take care of the girls. If any of you makes any disturbance, I am certainly going to see the sheriff."

To my relief, the two groups left in turn and soon disappeared. The three girls readily accepted the offer of a ride and we started out. A short way down the road, one of the girls exclaimed, "There are some boys waiting in the bushes. I'm scared!", but they were only their South River dates. I turned on the inside lights of the car so that the young men could see the girls, and they offered no interference. Thus, one more crisis passed with no ill feeling to worry about. I am sure that the couples were reunited within the hour but that was not my problem.

In view of the stress and strain under which these remarkable women worked, their patience was extraordinary, and so was their stamina. However, there was nothing superhuman about them, and, not seldom, the fitful contrariness of the people, whom the mission ladies were trying to mother, would become unbearable resulting in an emotional explosion all out of proportion to the cause. An example would be the case of a worker stationed at a very isolated mission. She had been practically confined to the house for weeks by heavy snows and bitter cold. Little mail got through. She had no radio and no telephone. The roads and paths were almost impassable. She saw few people except those in the immediate neighborhood of her station. Small wonder was it that she became nearly "stir crazy" in her little world. So also were the people living around her and they were as irritable as she was.

Finally, some minor insult from one of the women shattered her habitual dignity and forbearance. Without stopping to calm down, she wrote a letter of resignation to the church authorities to take effect at once, for she felt that she had had enough, and the next Sunday she announced to the people attending service that she was leaving right away. The neighborhood was shocked, for they really had the highest regard for her. They begged Mr. Luther, an influential man in that area, to go down to the mission and "reason with her." He did so and when she proved adamant, he demanded an explanation from her for abandoning her post without warning.

"The Lord is leading me to do so", she replied tartly.

"You better look out, ma'm," Mr. Luther warned. "Many's the time I thought the Lord was leading me to do things, but later I found 'twarn't nothing but the devil!" Happily the worker cooled down and changed her mind.

In addition to the regular workers, or veterans, there were the summer volunteers, mostly idealistic young women, who, having heard of the great need for helpers in the mountains when the weather would be open enough to permit extensive visiting, offered themselves for service. They were for the most part college students who felt that the least they could do would be to devote their vacations to really useful work. Such decisions usually threw their families into a panic. They conjured up horrendous pictures of what might happen to inexperienced girls in such wild and isolated areas from which flowed tales of violence, murder, and general lawlessness. Such fears were never justified, because these young women were treated with the utmost courtesy by the mountain folk.

The regulars generally awaited the arrival of these enthusiasts with feelings that were a mixture of interest and wariness. They did not object to working with these newcomers, for there was much hard work to be done and energetic assistance was more than welcome. The chief worry was whether or not these young people could stand the loneliness and primitiveness after the first flush of dedication wore off.

Here and there, a cynic might question their motives for wanting to come up into the Blue Ridge country. As an illustration, a young man had joined the staff of the Blue Ridge Industrial School, at Dyke, to serve as a lay reader for the summer, having just graduated from the University of Virginia. Not long after he had settled down, one of the women teachers of the romantic type once stopped him and said excitedly,

"Oh! I just heard some wonderful news. A nice young girl is coming out to work here this summer. She'll be here in a few days from Mary Washington College. Her name is Miss Constance Strobel. That's going to make it mighty pleasant for you now. Aren't you happy about it?"

His rather sour reply was, "I don't know about that. She's probably just a flapper looking for a new thrill!"

Unfortunately for him, this remark was repeated in due time to the young lady, who evened the score a bit in her efficient style. And well I know it, for I was the university graduate and the college girl became my wife in due time.

Volunteer mission workers and school teachers, new to the mountains, were subject to many surprises and novel experiences. The gentler the background from which they came, the sharper the jolt. One of these, just settled in her post, was visited by a young mountain wife who was curious about the "foreigner" and was not at all bashful about asking personal questions. During the conversation she inquired:

"How old be you?"

"Oh, maybe a little older than you."

"Then, how come you ain't kotched you a man yit?"

The mission ladies performed many valuable services for mountain people and especially for women. They were always on call, in times of trouble and sickness. The experienced ones were seldom startled by anything that happened, but the neophytes frequently were. One of these, answering a knock at the front door of the mission, found a young woman who asked the volunteer if she would kindly write a letter for her. Feeling complimented, she asked the visitor, whom she knew slightly, to come in. After writing materials were brought out, both sat down at the dining room table.

"Now, what do you want me to do?" asked the worker.

"Back the letter," replied the caller.

"What do you mean?"

"You know, write on the envellup who it's for and whar it's going."

This done, dictation began. The letter was to the woman's sister, who had moved away from the mountains, and consisted of family and neighborhood news. When there was a pause at last and the letter seemed to be at an end, the writer looked over her handiwork, taking pride in her beautiful script and in her best college English. Presently, she asked,

"Is there anything else you want me to write, Mrs. Becky?"

Where so many people had the same last name, such as Shifflett, Morris, Breeden, Snow, etc., it was quite usual to address them by their first names.

"Yes, ma'm," she replied. "Jest put down, 'please excuse the poor handwriting and bad spelling'."

The novice was devastated until a veteran explained that mountain etiquette demanded such an ending to a letter. Those who were literate were barely so in those days, and in the matter of handwriting and spelling, there was much to be desired.

By and large, these summer volunteers acquitted themselves well and won the respect not only of their co-workers but also of the people who observed them long and carefully before giving them their approval. Some of these young women in time returned to the mountains as mission workers or as school teachers. Others found husbands among the younger clergy, who were beginning their ministry in the Blue Ridge, or among the men involved in educational work. Most completed their education and made their homes and careers elsewhere. Now, no one runs to call for the Mission Lady, because great changes have eliminated the once dire need for her services, and Federal agencies have taken much of the field where years ago she was the main source of help for the mountaineer in time of trouble.

Chapter 3

BLOOD ON THE SPOTSWOOD TRAIL

U. S. 33, or that portion known as "The Spotswood Trail", is a useful but uninteresting thoroughfare for the average traveler coming from the east until he enters Greene County, where the Blue Ridge Mountains seem to rise up and spread out before his view. From here on and into the Valley of Virginia, the region has been described as "delightfully romantic" by sentimentalists who never lived there. This bit of fancy has long been accepted by native Virginians who were taught from early youth that this was the way Governor Alexander Spotswood came riding with his gallant band of "Knights of the Golden Horseshoe" in August, 1716, and spearheaded the westward expansion of Virginia into the Piedmont and Valley areas. Of late, certain scholastic heretics have spread the rumor that the noble Governor and his men never followed the route that bears his name but first viewed the Valley from some indefinite prominence farther to the north. But the true believers remain undisturbed and cling to what they were taught by their fathers, accepting every word of the record carved on the monument, which stands immovable and proud at Swift Run Gap, bearing mute testimony to the historic feat.

The climb over the mountains begins at Stanardsville, and the views which may please one from here are soon snuffed out by the ridges pressing close onto the highway until the crest is reached nine miles away. For over two hundred years, this stretch of the Spotswood Trail had been a miserable dirt road, rocky and tough, and travel over it was a nightmare at best for wayfarers. When at last, about two generations ago, the Trail was widened, graded and hard surfaced, it became a popular route, between the Piedmont country and the Valley. Legitimate traffic moved faster, but so did the lawless and the violent, making a three mile section between Cecil Memorial Chapel and Lydia a special plague spot until Prohibition was repealed by a disgusted nation. Violence was never absent, and no one felt really safe after nightfall.

Outrages were common, and they stemmed largely from the bootleg trade. The neighborhood of Lydia was the scene of many of them. Lydia was and still is a non-descript settlement lying on the north side of the highway, distinguished for nothing in particular. It was a squalid little collection of dwellings and a store that once doubled as a post office, none of which had been whitewashed or painted for decades. Opposite, south of the highway, rose the steep lower slopes of Turkey Ridge, dotted here and there with log homes and outbuildings, where families eked out a miserable living. The descriptive term "delightfully romantic" is nothing less than an imperious exercise of the imagination when applied to this three mile portion of the Spotswood Trail.

Matters were made worse by the Depression, two generations ago, when want was so severe that the need of getting money took precedence over how it was gotten. This is one reason why moonshining was resorted to on so wide a scale in view of the heavy demand for the product. Added to this was the fact that the young men had little or no work. Jobs were scarce. Numbers left the mountains to look for work in towns and cities, but most came back deeply discouraged and bitter. Time hung heavily on their hands. No one needed them. They had nowhere to go. They had nothing to do but to get into trouble.

In spite of the general lawlessness, Cecil Memorial Mission enjoyed comparative freedom from disturbances. The section was sparsely settled and the people were largely law abiding, hard working farmers. Yet one of the worst outbreaks in my missionary district occurred there during a lawn party.

Lawn parties were often held on the grounds in summertime and were very popular with the congregation. They were unexciting but pleasant events, bringing families together for a companionable evening in a community that had little social life of its own. They were looked on as occasions when a man could take his wife and family out for a good time without fearing for their safety. But good fortune ran out at one of them, which I was unable to attend.

This particular affair was going quite well when two separate carloads of men came down the Spotswood Trail at different times, and, seeing the festivities, decided to join the crowd. It so happened that each group was hostile to the other, and before long they met. A fight started and before it could be broken up, one of the Lydia men fell bleeding to the ground, badly sliced by a knife. The other combatants fled the scene abandoning the wounded man, who was succored by the local people. They rushed him to the hospital in Charlottesville where it took over sixty stitches to sew him up.

I was notified immediately and the next day, along with the sheriff, I went to the mission to investigate the affair. The Cecil people swarmed around expressing their indignation loudly and at great length. Presently, the sheriff was called away for another emergency, and, as he left, he told me:

"It's going to take more time than I got right now to get to the bottom of this mess. Suppose you get all the information you can and let me know. That bunch of no-goods are no strangers to me, but so far I can't figure out who is responsible. Really, they all are. They are nothing but Lydia trash. It happened on you all's land so it is up to you to swear out the warrants. I'll help you all I can."

When he left, the people swarmed around once more. They answered questions freely about who the men were, how the fight started, who did the knifing, and so on. They seemed gifted with total recall, and I listed at least two dozen who could testify in court. They also let me know that they fully expected me to see that justice was done and "put a stop to this here kind of devilment, else we can't bring our women and children no more at night to these here parties".

Several days later, when he could receive visitors, I interviewed the wounded man, hoping that he might give me some helpful information, but he was uncooperative. No, he did not know who cut him. No, he did not know who was in the car with him. "You see, we was all pretty drunk at the time". No, he didn't want to make trouble for anybody. So it went. But no matter, I had all the witnesses I needed and swore out warrants for all the hoodlums, the injured man included. The sheriff duly arrested them, and they were let out on bail until the patient would be well enough to attend a hearing.

In due time, they were rounded up and brought before the magistrates, who were to determine if there was enough evidence to send the case to the grand jury. In any event, there had been a breach of the peace on church grounds, and this was definitely within their jurisdiction. I had no worries, for I was certain that I had an open and shut case, and the commonwealth's attorney agreed with me after he had conferred with the eye-witnesses.

There is no such thing as a sure thing. The hearing was a disaster. My witnesses, one after the other, far from having total recall, now suffered a total loss of memory. Their testimony, such as it was, followed the same line. "There was a fight and it was terrible. There were so many folks milling around and hollering that a body couldn't rightly make out who was mixed up in it. A man nearly had his guts cut out but you couldn't see who did it." No specific details emerged.

The woman mission worker, who had so much at stake in the matter, could not help, though desperately anxious to do so. At the time, she was in the kitchen making coffee and had nothing to offer but hearsay. The lawyer for the defendants, who had pleaded not guilty, did not bother to put any witnesses on the stand. He asked that the case be dismissed for lack of evidence. But first, he made some choice remarks about a minister of the Gospel who had so little judgment as to have innocent people arrested and publicly humiliated solely on the basis of gossip. He trusted that I had learned my lesson and would proceed more carefully in the future. His heart bled for the injured man, assailant unknown, and hoped that the Episcopal churches would take proper measures hereafter to ensure the safety of those who attended their public gatherings.

The magistrates retired to the jury room. In a short while, the deputy sheriff came for me and said that the magistrates wanted to talk with me privately. I followed him wondering what there was to say after such a fiasco. The presiding magistrate came to the point as soon as we sat down:

"We are going to have to let those men go, much as we would like to see them get what they deserve. You weren't at the party. The mission lady didn't see the fight. We just don't have any evidence that would stand up five minutes. All your witnesses went back on you. Don't take it too bad. It has happened before and it will happen again. Your witnesses didn't forget anything. They just remembered something else too well. I don't say they were suborned, but I'll bet my bottom dollar that word got to them one way or another, that if they wanted to stay healthy and not have bad luck, the more they disremembered the better off they would be. None of them wanted to be bushwhacked, or to have cows shot, or to have barns burn down. So they let you down. We are sorry. You and your church are doing a lot of good in this county and we want to back you all we can. In this sorry business, all we can do is wish you better luck."

This was cold comfort, but from that time on, there was peace at Cecil Memorial Mission.

For some strange reason, eruptions of disorder at my churches usually occurred while I was preaching. The only explanation seemed to be that when the congregations gathered for worship, they gathered slowly and stood around outside a church for sociability and gossip until time to go in. When the bell rang, the women and girls and very young children would go in first; then the men and the younger boys next; finally, the older boys and the young men under twenty-five would straggle in, except for a few who remained outdoors for a while longer to show their independence. These latter were the material out of which commotions flared. Before sermon time, there was a period long enough for anger to heat up to flash point from ridicule or an insult. But not always. Once at Jewel Chapel, Lydia, trouble started in church right in front of me, while I was in the pulpit.

Hardly had I begun my sermon, when the front door opened and two seventeen year old boys, followed by a much younger one, came in and sat in a back pew behind three girls. In a moment or two, the older youths leaned over and began annoying them. The girls promptly got up and moved ahead a pew. The three boys moved up and repeated the performance. The girls moved again and so did the boys. At this point I thought that matters had gone far enough, so I ordered the boys to leave the building, and repeated the command for emphasis. They looked up startled but stayed where they were. Temper took over then, and I rushed out of the pulpit toward them. There was a brief flash of worry about what to do if they stood their ground but the trio grabbed their hats and shot out of the door. After that it was difficult to continue the service but we managed somehow.

When the congregation had been dismissed, I conferred with Mr. Freeman J. Fisk, the lay preacher in charge of the mission, about whether or not some action should be taken about the matter, but we decided to put it in the "boys will be boys" file and forget it. Taking leave of the lingering members of the congregation and of the caretaker, Tom Lamb, I drove home, still bothered about the incident, fearing that light handling might encourage further misbehavior. Tom Lamb and his family lived in a small house provided by the mission, situated across the lane on the front of the church,

Hardly had I gotten home, when the phone rang. It was the lay reader, his voice quivering with anger:

"Those boys! ... Those rotten boys! . . Right after you chased them out of the church, they broke into the Lamb's kitchen. Now listen to what they did. They killed the two cats, they broke the chairs to pieces, they broke every jar of the preserves and vegetables that Mrs. Lamb had put up, they poured out three crocks of milk and clabber all over the floor, and smashed the crocks. There is other damage, but what I told you is bad enough. Mrs. Lamb is just about hysterical, and I don't blame her. You know how poor the family is, and they can't stand the loss of all that food. We have got to help the Lambs replace it and the furniture. Mr. Lamb says that if we don't have those boys punished, he's going to lay for them and settle with them his way."

"Do you know the names of the boys?" I asked him.

"Yes, I know them. They don't live far from here."

"Well, come on down to Stanardsville tomorrow with all the information you have," I directed. "Meet me at the courthouse and I'll swear out the warrants. We can't do anything tonight except to help the Lambs."

It took the better part of the week for the sheriff to catch the culprits. The late spring weather was warm and pleasant, so the boys made a sport of dodging through the woods, over the hills, and in the hollows. Ultimately, hunger and weariness drove them out, and they were promptly apprehended. Then the vexing question came up again: how hard to be on these youngsters in view of their youth? I could not accept the responsibility of asking for prison terms or even that they be sent to reform school. Happily, in my term of service, matters never went that far. The best policy seemed to be the one suggested by a mountaineer, "Make 'em pay for it."

The trio was brought before the magistrates as quickly as possible, since in small affairs speedy trial and speedy punishment usually made a strong impression and toned down high spirits. The two older ones pleaded guilty but asked the magistrates to let the younger one go because neither in church nor the break-in did he have any real part in what happened. They admitted that it looked bad for the youngster, Clark, to be "dodging" with them, but Clark was tagging along for the fun of it until he got hungry and homesick. So Clark was released but the other two were fined and ordered to pay full damages to the Lambs for the loss they suffered, which of course were paid by the parents of the pair.

All parties were satisfied with the settlement. The families of the boys were grateful that the church did not "make it hard" for their sons. The Lambs were able to restock their larder and to replace destroyed furniture and other articles. The community was happy that "wild young folks" were shown that such foolishness cost more than it was worth. As for the church there was peace at Jewel Chapel for a season, but not for long, as it turned out.

Jewel Chapel no longer exists, as the property was incorporated into the Shenandoah National Park. The name came from a gift that made its construction possible. A devout lady in New York heard of the dire need of a church in the Lydia area with resident workers to staff it, and responded by making a gift of some of her jewelry to meet it. It was sold and the mission was established. Regardless of some untoward happenings, a considerable service, social as well as religious, was rendered to the community, which amply justified the venture.

The last serious incident at Jewel Chapel during my stay created a situation that for a while had elements of danger. It happened early on a summer evening, when June was at its loveliest. The clear skies in the west glowed with the colors of sunset, and sweet smelling breezes made going indoors seem almost a sacrilege. But the congregation had gathered and was anxious for the service to start. The continuous threat of disorder kept the people nervous, and it was their wish that the service should begin at sundown so that afterward they could head homewards before it got "too dark", since the twilight lingered long at that time of year. Though the front doors of the church were closed, the windows were all open, dispelling the stuffiness characteristic of little churches that have been closed all week.

The service proceeded without incident and all seemed well until the time came for the sermon. Scarcely had I begun my address, when suddenly outside there were shrieks and a woman's voice screamed, "Oh, my God, folks! We got a dead man out here! What are we doing to do? There's a dead man here!"

With that, the people started up from their seats and began to mill around the nave in a panic. I came down out of the pulpit and with great difficulty quieted them enough to get their attention. Yet, I felt almost as alarmed as they did since the shrieking continued.

"Listen all of you," I shouted above the hubbub. "Sit down! Sit down!"

When they finally did so, I continued,

"I don't know what has happened, but I'll go out and see. Now you stay right in here until I find out what's going on. You men, look after the women and children and keep them quiet. Don't go outside now. If I need you, I'll call you. For now, stay where you are."

Then I went through the doors and looked around. The twilight was fading, but the exterior light above the entrance of the church gave considerable illumination. All I could see was a hysterical woman dancing around in a circle, wringing her hands and wailing over and over, "There's a dead man here! What are we going to do?" I recognized her as Mrs. Beulah who lived a short distance up the road, which ran along outside the stone fence enclosing the mission property. There was no sign of a body. In fact, there was no sign of anybody else at all. So I went down the steps and tried to get some information from her but to no avail. She was wildly emotional. I could not get her attention, even though I grabbed her by the arms and shook her.

Giving up, I began to look around to discover what had upset her without result until I saw a face peering around the back corner of the caretaker's in front of the church. Though it was dusk, I would know that ferret-like face anywhere, and I also knew that where the owner was, there was probably trouble. It belonged to an undersized youth who had been grossly mis-nicknamed Sheepie. He was a sneak; cunning, mean, and not to be trusted behind you. The only way he deserved his nickname was that he tagged along after those of his peers who were tall and muscular, helling and drinking with them, getting a vicarious satisfaction out of their extralegal exploits and feeling that he was as good as any man as long as he was in their company. He was suspected of urging his less intelligent heroes into many fights and not a few cutting scrapes, yet somehow not getting involved directly, thus keeping just out of the reach of the sheriff, who would have liked nothing more than to have a legal reason for throwing Sheepie into jail along with the semi-thugs on whom he fawned so much.

So I headed in that direction and, arriving at the back of the house, found enough to keep me busy for a while. In the dusk, I could make out an assemblage of about eight to ten people sitting on some of the rocks that dotted the grounds and whose attention was centered on three persons. The center one was cursing and waving his arms while the other two were holding on to him and trying to calm him down. Moving on by Sheepie and one or two others of his ilk to the trio, I recognized the shouter as Robert, the strapping son of Mrs. Beulah, whose screams first sounded the alarm, and the ones trying to pacify him were his two sisters. They were getting no help from the fascinated audience. As soon as he saw me, for I still had my vestments on, Robert became quiet, breathing hard.

"Robert, your mother said a man was hurt. Where is he?" I asked.

"Thar he is," replied Robert pointing to the ground.

I looked down and saw a still form. I was almost standing on him. I knelt down for a better look at the person. He was lying flat on his back, except for his right forearm, which was erect from the elbow and motionless but for the hand that was jerking spasmodically from right to left. I looked at the face and saw that it was a young man, whom I only knew as Herbert. His parents were dead and he lived with his grandfather three miles up the mountain but was seldom home since he drifted about the area with his servile band of bullies, much to the annoyance of the populace which despised him more than they feared him.

Standing up, I asked, "What happened?"

"He called me a bad name and I hit him," Robert replied.

Someone verified it.

"Yes, he called him a real bad name. Herbert had no business picking a fight 'cause Robert is much more of a man than he is."

"Never mind," I responded "This is bad business. Herbert looks in bad shape. What did you hit him with, Robert?"

"I hit him with my fist," Robert said. I felt relieved but only for a moment. "No, that ain't so. I busted him in the head with a rock."

I knelt down again and, in the dark, felt about Herbert's head. My hand came away bloody. Wiping my hand on the grass, I was pondering what to do next, when happily Herbert began to come to and presently sat up. It might have been better to have kept him quiet for a while longer but he was insistent and I wanted to get him to the light to see the extent of his injury. So with the help of one of the bystanders, we started to the front of the church. Before leaving I said to Robert and his sisters, "I want you to go home right away. You girls see that he gets home and stays home. I'll talk to him later on in a day or so. But just now I must take care of Herbert. Go home right now!"

In front of the church, under the light, the wound did not seem to be serious and the bleeding had stopped. Herbert seemed to be coming around all right but was quite dizzy. Just then there was a sound of alarm from those standing around and from the part of the congregation that had ventured out on the steps. Looking about I saw Robert coming up spoiling to renew the fight. His sisters were hanging on to him, pleading with him to leave, but he was shoving them away. In a moment, I found myself holding on to Robert's shirt front with one hand and on to Herbert's with the other, holding them apart as best I could. I called to the men to help but no one stirred. At this juncture, Robert's father appeared. He put his arms around his son, dragged him away and literally pushed him up the road to where the family lived.

It was imperative to get Herbert away from the place before anything worse happened. So getting hold of Sheepie and one of the other youths, we put Herbert in my car, and I drove them up the highway to the path along which they could get Herbert to his grandfather's cabin without much trouble.

Before they left, I told Herbert and his friends that 1 wanted to see Herbert at my house in Stanardsville the next Thursday to talk over the affair because he had a part in breaking up a church service and I could not overlook it. Though Herbert was still somewhat woozy, he said that he understood and would be there.

I drove back to the church and found that the congregation had not left, most of them remaining in the building, being afraid to go home. I told them that I thought that they should get started before it got much later. Then I went to the back room to change my clothes. I removed my vestments, packed them in my bag and got ready to depart. Half way down the aisle, I was almost run over by people stampeding back into the building. Someone was shouting:

"Oh, My God! Here he comes back again. He's got a pistol! He's got a pistol!"

The men were useless before and certainly would not be of any help now. I knew only too well that I was responsible for commanding and keeping the peace around the church and that whatever had to be done, I would have to do it. I dropped my bag and went outside. The exterior light was strong enough for me to see beyond the stone fence. There was Robert coming down the road to the driveway gate, followed by his sisters, his mother and father, all calling to him to come back and make no more trouble. I got to the gate before they arrived and latched it, feeling that Robert had to be met there. As he came close, I was vastly relieved to see no sign of a pistol either in his hand or on his person. When he arrived, he saw that I was holding the gate shut and he stopped. He made no move, so I thought that I had the upper hand. We stared at each other for a minute or two, and then I said:

"Robert, I told you to go home and stay there, but here you are again. You have made trouble enough for one night. Why did you come back?"

I'm looking for Herbert. He called me a dirty name, and I've got to settle it with him," he replied.

"Herbert isn't here. I drove him up the road and he has gone home", I told him. "You are in a lot of trouble now and I have plenty of witnesses if I want to make you pay for it. I can't put up with this kind of behavior and you know it. You and I now have something to settle between us. I want you at my house in Stanardsville early Tuesday to talk it over. That will give us both time to cool off. See that you get there."

Then I turned to his father,

"Robert is young, and I don't want to give him a bad reputation but he has too hot a temper for his own good. I can have him arrested, but I want to settle this business as peaceably as I can. Now, you get him home and keep him home. See that he comes to see me Tuesday without fail. If he makes any more trouble, I'll just have to send the sheriff after him. Understand?"

He nodded and took his son by the arm and they moved off home, followed by the rest of the family. Going back to the church, I told the people to get going as quickly as possible, and that I would stay until they got a reasonable distance from the church. They needed no further urging. After a while, I left also.

On the way home, I was troubled about the way I handled the affair, so I stopped off to talk it over with the sheriff.

"Why did you tell them to come down and talk to you?" he asked.

"Well, I don't want to have those boys arrested if I can help it," I told him. "They have to walk six miles to town and six miles back. That will give them time to think things over and know that I am not taking it lightly. If they are reasonable, I'll be satisfied. Anyway, I want you to know what happened in case the business goes any farther."

"I am glad you did," he said. "You did what you thought was right but I think that you are wrong—about Robert, anyhow. He won't come down. Herbert will. He's not vicious like Robert, and I look for him to settle down before long. I know he's kind of wild but he's stupid, yet he'll turn out all right. Now Robert is as mean as a snake. You won't have to worry about him long. One of these days, somebody is going to put a bullet right between his eyes, and it will be good riddance. Call on me if you need me."

The sheriff was wrong on every count as it turned out. Very early on Tuesday morning, I was awakened by a banging on my front door. Putting on a robe, I came down to see what it was all about, and there was Robert. I invited him in and we had a long friendly discussion. He was most apologetic and promised to make no more trouble at church. Before he left, he noticed some magazines on my reading table and asked if I had any old ones to spare, saying that they never had a magazine at home to look at and he wanted to see what they were like.

I gave him several for which he thanked me profusely. We shook hands, and he went on his way.

Herbert however did not show up on Thursday nor the rest of the week. This created a problem, for if I let one off, it would be difficult to hail the other into court and have a case. There was nothing to do but to try a bluff. I sent him word by one of the Lydia people that if I did not see him soon, I would go and see the sheriff. The result was that, a few days later, he and Sheepie were banging at my door at a very early hour. I learned that "early" to a mountaineer meant soon after sunrise. He had a black eye and his head was bandaged. He insisted that he had no recollection at all of the fight nor my telling him that I wanted to see him. I believed Herbert. Sheepie's memory was defective also. I didn't believe him. The conversation was not very satisfactory. I got a promise of good behavior but no apology, so I let it go at that.

Later that summer Herbert and his rat pack were on one of their nuisance tours in the area. Their wandering took them by the cabin of a widowed mountaineer whose only child was a mentally retarded son about sixteen years of age. The boy was usually alone during the day as his father had a job at a sawmill. Herbert, knowing that the boy would be by himself, would stop by now and then to tease and to threaten to harm the youngster, who became terrified of him. This day, the boy saw Herbert and his gang coming down the road, and, fearing another visit, got ready for it. As usual, Herbert, seeing the boy on the porch, decided to have some fun with him. As he walked up the path to the house, the lad reached inside the door for a shotgun, which he had just loaded, and fired at point blank range, killing Herbert instantly.

About a year later, I was once more awakened early by a loud banging on the rectory door. Putting on a robe, I went down and opened the door. Once again, there stood Robert, but this time he had a freckled faced girl, about his age, with him.

"Robert, what in the world brings you two around here at the crack of dawn?" I asked with some surprise.

"We want you to marry us. Will you do it?" he asked, blushing beet red.

"Come on in," I invited. "You two have got to give me time to dress and to wake up my wife and a house guest and give them time to dress too. You have to have two witnesses to make it legal, you know. Where is the license?"

He produced it and after the proper preparations were made, they exchanged their vows and departed with a blessing. The sheriff was right in one respect, perhaps. Robert was no longer a worry to anyone. Instead of a mountain bullet, his mountain belle quickly got him in hand and gentled him down.

Chapter 4

NOW EXPLAIN THAT TO ME

Like all lay people, the mountain folk are not hesitant about instructing their ministers concerning his duties according to their lights. The members of Saddle Back Mission were convinced that I was sent there not only to preach the Gospel, but also to police the morals of the mountain, provided, of course, that I did not meddle too close to home. Accordingly, at first, some of them began to "name it" to me that I should go and visit Milt Allen and see if I could persuade him to mend his ways, because he was a "mighty wicked man". Sometime before, I had learned that the term "wicked" could signify almost anything, but mainly it meant that a person "cusses and sw'ars" immoderately. I was fairly well acquainted with Milt and had not noticed that his vocabulary was overloaded in this respect. However, when irritated enough, Milt could acquit himself with distinction, but gossip did not point to him as a blasphemer more notorious than others of his ilk. So seeing no urgency about this matter, I let it slide.

As time went on, the faithful "named it" to me more frequently and with greater insistence. It was also pointed out to me that I was losing influence and was getting the reputation of being a preacher who did not seem to care that "the devil was running hog wild on the mountain and that people were going to hell all over". Finally, it became quite plain that I had to do something. The immediate task was to ascertain the precise nature of his alleged moral turpitude. This was not easy, since the people were very close-mouthed about some things. There was always the possibility of suffering some harm to person or property from talking too much about other folk's business.

When, at last, I ran down the nature of the accusation, it was a letdown. Milt was a moonshiner. So what was so unusual about that? At least a third of my members were suspected of being involved in the "likker" traffic one way or another, even including a few of those who were insisting that I should go and reason with Milt Allen. The rub was this: it wasn't the moonshining so much as the fact that Milt's place was too wide open in its operations. A number of his customers would consume his product on the premises and lie around drunk for days. He appeared to have a large clientele, many coming from some distance to patronize him. It was reported that there was quarreling, fighting, and other deviltry in the woods nearby. Noisy drunks molested travelers at times as they went up and down the road. All this was offensive enough, but chief concern was expressed over the bad influence such "carryings-on" would have on the young people, who in time might well be drawn into these activities.

Being rather callow in those days and eager "to do my duty", I set off on this mission at last, though without much enthusiasm for it. There is always the suspicion of being trapped into pulling other people's chestnuts out of the fire and then being left alone to take the consequences if anything goes wrong. Why didn't the people themselves complain to the authorities? Well, it just wasn't safe, and the result could be unpleasant if the accused decided to get even, as was often the case. But I was a "foreigner" and could get away with it, or so it was assumed.

I started out early on a beautiful July morning. It had rained hard the night before, and by dawn the skies had cleared to a deep blue, without a cloud in sight. Visibility was almost perfect in all directions. Driving six miles along the gravel county road, I came to the turnoff onto the clay road that led up the mountain. I did not get far, because the heavy rain had turned what was really a wagon trail into a quagmire, and the car bogged down within a hundred yards. Throwing rocks and brush under the back wheels, I managed to back down to the intersection, where the hard-packed roadbed could be depended upon. It was plain that I would not get up to Milt's place by car that day. This was not the first time I had run into this trouble, and early in my ministry I had made arrangements to meet such a contingency.

So I drove to the farm of Herbert Holt, who lived about half a mile away. He and I had a business arrangement, agreed upon after much discussion whereby he would rent me a horse for fifty cents a day, if he had one to spare, which fortunately was the case this particular day. In the beginning, he wanted to let me have the use of the horse free of charge, " 'cause I like to help people doing the Lord's work". Those were the Depression years and, after considerable argument, he gave in but vowed that he would not take a penny more than fifty cents, "to pay for the oats I'll give you to feed the horse the first good chance you have after you get whar your business is".

At that time, I was relieved that he would even talk to me about a horse because I was well aware that he "did not favor 'Piscopal preachers none". Later on, when we had established a good relationship, he told me the nature of his complaint:

"A good while back, one of your kind of folks was around here, preaching on your circuit, I won't name him. I liked him real well, and I done him many a favor. But one day, he went down to Richmond to some church meeting to try and get hold of some money for what he was aiming to do in these parts. He talked mighty rough about the folks up here, how ignorant and poor we all were. But the worst thing was that he gave me a bad name. Yes, sir, he named me by name. It got into the papers, and the people up here read all about it. It was hard to stand after all I did for him. I'll get over it some day, I reckon, and I guess that if he ever would need me, I'd help him."

The mission work always needed money, and the workers spent a great deal of time on speaking trips. There was the continual temptation to use the "bleeding heart" approach and to employ spectacular illustrations. Names were apt to creep in, unfortunately, when the speakers got carried away by the rapt attention of the listeners. Most of the time, there was little danger in such an unwise practice, because reporters seldom were present, but when there happened to be such unflattering publicity, mountain resentment was keen and the damage was difficult to repair. However, in this case, hostility did not extend to me, and this form of transportation was always available.

Soon, Mr. Herbert had a good riding horse saddled, and the rations for the trip in a gunny sack were tied to the saddle. After parking my car under a large oak tree beside the farm house, I set out again on my mission. Nearing the turnoff, I overtook one Pleasant Dunnivan, who was on his way to the store. He greeted me with some effusiveness and evidently had more time to talk than I. We passed the time of day, and he told me to be very careful going up the mountain because he heard that the storm had done a lot of damage by blowing down limbs and trees and that some parts of the road had been washed out. Seeing that I had to move on, he gave me a hearty goodbye and went on his way.

Pleasant had not always been so lavish in his display of friendship. The change in his attitude dated back to a night several months ago, when I was awakened by someone calling under my bedroom window: "Hey in there. Somebody open up. I want to come in out of this cold and visit a spell." Looking out of the window, I could see that it was Pleasant, since there was a full moon. Going downstairs and putting on an overcoat, I went outdoors to see what the trouble was, after closing the door behind me.

"What are you doing here?" I asked

"Just thought I'd stop by for a visit," he answered.

"Three o' clock in the morning is no time to be paying visits."

"I'm sort of confused. Whose house is this, anyway?"

"It's the Episcopal minister's house. You ought to know me."

"I sho am mixed up. Don't know how I got here. Kin I come in and talk with you some?"

"Look here, Pleasant, you are as drunk as you can be. Now you sit down on the edge of the porch and I'll get dressed and drive you home before you get into real trouble."

"Don't do that. My wife'll kill me. Let me stay here, 'till I sober up."

"No, you belong home. Stay right here now until I get ready. Don't move. I'll only be a minute or two", I instructed, and he sat down grumbling about the lack of neighborliness. In a short while, I drove him out to the South River Road to his gate but had a difficult time getting rid of him. He wanted to stay in the car and talk until "sunup", he said. The only thing that moved him was my threat to go to the house and tell his family that I needed help to get him in since it looked like he was too drunk to walk. In a moment he was on his way to his door. What passed between him and his wife, I never knew, but from that night on his manner toward me was exceptionally cordial whenever we met.

In a few minutes after my chance meeting with Pleasant, the ascent of the mountain began. There was no travel on the road, and all the activity I saw was provided by numerous chipmunks, an occasional rabbit, flocks of birds and two deer. When we reached the Split Rock, it was time to rest the horse, and this afforded an opportunity to look around. It was not high enough for much of a view, but I was glad to note that there was not as much damage to the trees as Pleasant reported. So far, nowhere was the road blocked.

Looking down a small valley to the left, I could just make out the roof of old Joel Shifflett's house and couldn't help laughing. Two weeks before, I was sent a message by Joel's family that he was dying and would I come as quick as I could. Many times I had received similar messages but usually found out that a person reported at death's door was only mildly sick. Isolated families panicked easily in times of illness. But this message sounded urgent, so I dropped everything, drove out as near to Joel's place as I could, and walked a quarter of a mile to the back of his house unobserved and, through the kitchen window, to my surprise, I could see Joel fully dressed, standing by the kitchen stove, smoking his pipe.

To see what would happen, I called out, "Anybody home?" Through the window a sudden flurry of activity was visible, and in a few minutes his son came out and invited me to come in and visit with his father who was "mighty bad off". Going in, I found the old man lying in bed very still and with his eyes shut tight. The covers were pulled up high, practically to his nose—too high in fact—because in the rush there was no time to get his shoes off, and there they were in full view, to the embarrassment of his family. I went along with the farce as well as I could with no offense. Joel was getting feeble and had a bad heart, so any sign of ill health was apt to be exaggerated by his family. Then too, these isolated people were glad to have any excuse to get attention to relieve their loneliness. They really had my sympathy.

The horse indicated that he had rested long enough, and so the journey was resumed. The higher we climbed the more exquisite the view became. The finest overlook was at the B'ar Stand, near Milt Allen's place, where I stopped to rest the horse again and enjoyed the scenery. That spot was named the B'ar Stand, because, in time gone by, it was on the route that bears followed going from Saddle Back toward High Top. Here they usually paused for a while on their journey. Here also hunters would lie in wait for them as they stopped and hunted for food. In my day, few were left to furnish easy targets for so-called sportsmen who slaughtered the animals from ambush. However, in recent years, bears appear to have increased in numbers under the protection of the Shenandoah National Park.

It was time to move on, and all too soon the opening was reached where a trail led down to Milt's house. Arriving, everything was quiet, not even a dog was around to herald my coming. Tethering the horse to the rail fence, I feared that I had made my trip for nothing, since there was no way to notify him in advance of my intended visit. I walked around to the front of the house and there was my quarry sitting in a rocking chair on the porch, smoking his pipe, and seeming to be very much at peace with the world.

Milt was quite surprised to see me, but his welcome was very warm. Getting another rocking chair from within the house, he invited me to sit and visit with him. No one else was home. Mrs. Allen, he said, was away visiting a sick friend. The boys had taken the dogs into the woods to see if they could find a 'coon. So Milt declared that he was glad to have some company that morning and, as etiquette demanded, he hoped that I would stay all day. Yet, I could see that he was wondering why I was there.

We talked of this and that for a while and admired the rare quality of the view from his porch, for seldom in the Blue Ridge was the air so clear. We could see Charlottesville clearly, and from our vantage point pick out a few of the larger buildings. We were interested in spotting the street cars (long since things of the past now), and at times on their routes sunlight was reflected from their roofs and windows. It wasn't often, Milt said, that the city was so visible, but many times at night it was a pretty sight all lighted up.

Anon, the time came to get down to the business I had come for. All the journey up the mountain I had organized my speech and delivered it as planned, being frank that I was well informed about his occupation and the concern it caused his neighbors, pointing out the dangers of lawlessness that created so much trouble in the county, expatiating on the temptations placed in the way of young people to their detriment, and urging him to turn to better ways of earning a livelihood, and so on until I exhausted my theme.

All the while, Milt listened gravely and courteously, smoked his pipe, stared off into the distance, and murmured a "That's so?" or a "So they say", from time to time. When I had obviously ended my homily, he got up from his chair, walked to the edge of the porch, knocked the dottle from the pipe, filled it with his home grown and cured tobacco, returned to his chair, relighted the pipe; and, after several puffs, began to have his say.

"Now, Mr. Ribble, I done listened to you real close and don't take no harm for the things you said. You mean well, being a preacher and all. It's your business to set things straight, like you see it. You tell me that I make and sell likker. I does. I admits it. I ain't going to tell you no lie about it. You tell me that I do wrong.

"Now, I'm a ignorant man. I ain't never had much l'arning. Had no chance. Now you are a high-up educated man and you know a heap more than I know or ever will know. You say that I break the law and do wrong. You may be right, because you know so much. Well, I'm going to ask you to explain something to me."

Taking his pipe out of his mouth, Milt pointed southward with the stem, and resumed:

"Thar's Charlottesville out thar. They tell me that it's a real nice city. I ain't never been thar. Too many people, and it ain't got nothing that I got to go for and fetch back. Now, they tells me that they got a university down thar. Is that so?"

I confirmed his information.

Milt nodded and continued: "Now, they tell me that in that university they got a law school. Is that right?"

I agreed.

"Now, I hear tell that in the law school they teach people what is right and what is wrong. Is that so?"

"Yes", I replied. "What is right and what is wrong according to the law of the land."

41

"Then", he said triumphantly, slapping his hand down on the flat arm of his rocking chair, "You tell me that I do wrong! But these are the very people who come 'way out here and ask me to sell 'em likker!! Now explain that to me!"

There wasn't much left to say—at least I couldn't think of anything. Milt invited me to stay and eat "a mess" because the "old lady" would be back soon and "fix some vittles". But somehow my appetite had lost its edge, so I pleaded the press of some unfinished business down home and took my leave. All the long ride down the mountain, I pondered this new lesson and concluded that I still had much to learn about these people.

Chapter 5

Edgar
THE STORY OF A LOSER

Edgar Morris, hurt in his pride and feeling persecuted by his enemies, seethed with anger as he thought of the injustices he had to endure. Here he was on this twenty-ninth day of March, 1919, sitting alone in the office of the Clerk of Greene County and told to stay there by his father and by his lawyer until they sent word to him to come over to the courthouse where the magistrates would shortly consider a warrant charging him with attending a church meeting carrying a concealed weapon. He wasn't the only one there with a pistol. It wasn't fair. He had already been tried on that charge and fined twenty dollars by two of the three magistrates of the county. The third, Bluford G. Sullivan, or Son Sullivan, as he was called, was not at the first hearing and was now asking to have the case reopened because he thought that the punishment was too light and wanted to argue about it. That was just like him, always butting into other folk's business, especially Edgar's. Sullivan was always hounding him and hitting him with warrants for fighting and disturbing the peace. Gossip reached him that Son vowed that if Edgar didn't change his ways, he might have to use his gun to calm Edgar down. This made him especially angry, because Son was always giving him a bad name and turning people against him.

Edgar realized that he would have to admit if pushed that there were reasons for folks thinking him lawless and dangerous. Right then, as he was being summoned before the magistrates, he was out of jail on a

$5,000 bond, put up by his father, for shooting and seriously wounding his cousin, James Morris, at a dance and was due to appear in court April 21. It wasn't his fault Jim was shaming him before everybody and wouldn't shut up, so there wasn't anything else to do but to draw on him. Nobody could talk to him like that and expect him to take it. Folks just didn't understand. If they didn't like him, they should stand aside when they saw him coming. He had his buddies and didn't need anybody else. He wasn't wanted at churches and dances, but he wasn't to blame for all the things they told on him. Yes, he did carry a concealed weapon to church that time. When a man has so many people down on him, he had to look out for himself. As a matter of fact, he had two pistols concealed on him right then, law or no law. It was just as well that his father didn't know about it, because his father was Deputy Sheriff of the county and would take them off him, just when he needed them. Edgar was sure that Son Sullivan was the cause of most of his troubles and would shoot him down if he had half of an excuse. He himself had let it be known that he would shoot Sullivan if Son gave the slightest sign that he might draw on him. This is why his father and lawyer kept him sitting in the clerk's office like a bad child who couldn't be trusted to behave. Edgar's mood was getting worse the longer he was kept waiting and had time to remember the ways he was mistreated. Last year he had volunteered for the army and four months later the army kicked him out. They said that he wasn't fit to be a soldier because he was "inadaptable", whatever that was.

Edgar got up and looked out the window. It was cold and stormy out there, which was the way he felt. Why hadn't they called him? He wasn't going to stay here much longer. A man ought to take care of his own business. Those two old men said that they could compromise the case better for him if he stayed away until they got it settled. But they weren't going to settle it the way he wanted it settled. He saw Herman Shifflett waiting for him outside, back from carrying the mail between Stanardsville and Bacon Hollow. Herman had told Edgar he had a pistol and would stand by him if there was any trouble. Herman was a good friend even if he was only eighteen years old compared to Edgar's twenty-two.

Edgar lit a cigarette and went back to his chair and brooded morbidly about his situation, his hatred for Son Sullivan growing the while. He piled all his disappointments, frustrations, resentments, all that messed up his life, on the broad shoulders of Bluford C. Sullivan and wildly imagined that if he could get shed of Son Sullivan, he would get rid of everything that pestered him. He watched a group leave the clerk's office. He knew them. They knew him. The boy and girl were going to get married and they had just gotten their license. Their parents and some kinfolks were with them giggling and joking. They looked squarely at him and did not even speak. This was the kind of thing Son had done to him – turned people against him. This couldn't go on no matter what advice his father and lawyer gave him for keeping out of Sullivan's way. Sullivan had it in for him. There would be no peace and no safety as long as Sullivan was alive. It couldn't go on. Putting on his hat and overcoat, he jerked the office door open and went out into the gale. He signaled Herman to join him, and, after a hurried conference, both entered the courthouse.

Herman stayed by the door, and Edgar moved on down the aisle and took a seat behind his father. Attendance on the magistrates' court was rather sparse because of the weather, and scarcely anyone noticed either one at this point. Justice Sullivan was addressing the two magistrates who were giving their colleague their full attention as he discussed a point of law while consulting a law book which he held in his hand.

Suddenly, Edgar half rose holding a pistol in each hand, leaned over his father's shoulder and quickly fired six shots at his enemy. One shot knocked the law book out of Sullivan's hand. One struck him in the center of his forehead, and the rest found their mark in his body, which instantly crumpled lifeless to the floor.

Edgar reloaded his pistols with a coolness bordering on contempt, and, daring the horrified spectators to follow him, made his way to the door and out the building. Herman covered Edgar's deliberate exit by waving his pistol and ordering the stunned audience to stay where they were. He also fired some shots for emphasis. Then he left. Edgar easily made his escape. Possible pursuers were disorganized and unnerved by the dreadful outrage that they had just witnessed. Some of the bolder spirits did venture outside in a few moments. Herman was not in sight, and Edgar was seen going up to the cemetery nearby. There he paused and shouted insults and threats of harm to anyone who came after him. Some said that Edgar waved a Winchester rifle to back up his bluster.

Later, no one seemed to remember the rifle. Until the first shock wore off, every report was suspect. By the time Sheriff Malone got a posse organized, Edgar was long gone, leaving in his wake rumors of the wildest sort. No one even seemed to know which way he started his flight, if it can be called a flight since a few observers saw him going through Mutton Hollow toward the hills at a walk. His whereabouts became a mystery that lasted thirty-three days. The posse combed the hills and hollows and never found a trace of their quarry. Many assumed that he was being hidden by relatives, and since there were over five hundred Morrises in the county, this theory seemed plausible until Edgar's trial, when it was learned that he had made his way through the Valley of Virginia to Tennessee, Kentucky, and into West Virginia where he worked in lumber camps. Eighteen year old Herman, on the other hand, was speedily caught and jailed.

From the time of Edgar's escape, a pall of terror lay over the area, and rumors multiplied making the search very difficult for the sheriff and his men. There were fears that Edgar, a desperate man, would slip back and even some scores. There were complaints that while the pursuit dragged on day after day, the people were without protection, and it was urged that the governor of the State be petitioned to request that Federal troops be sent in to take up the hunt which seemed to be beyond the powers of the local officers. Such troops would be the very ones who could reassure the citizens of the region now quaking under the rumored threats of a ruthless ruffian. The longer the search went on unsuccessfully, the more the public mood verged on panic.

The extent of it is revealed by a headline in The Richmond Times Dispatch on April 21, 1919:

> STANARDSVILLE ARMED CAMP AS STATE
> SOLDIERS AWAIT RAID BY KLANSMAN
>
> TROOPERS PATROL COURTHOUSE YARD
> TO DEFEAT MORRIS

There was no raid, and the soldiers went home the next day. The regular session of the Circuit Court was scheduled to meet April 21. It was reported that Edgar had sent word down from the mountains that he would shoot up the Court if it convened to consider his case. The State authorities ordered the Albemarle Rifles of Charlottesville to Stanardsville to guard the Court in case trouble did develop. Since there was still a panicky mood, even though Edgar did not appear with friends, the same military company was held in readiness in case the Greene County Sheriff called for help before the work of the Court was finished. The grand jury duly indicted Edgar Morris for murder. Also, since Edgar did not appear for trial, his bond was forfeited, and his father was ruined financially as he was a man of very modest means.

Other things beside fear disturbed the peace of the village and county. For one thing, there was shame that such a crime could be committed in a God-fearing community. Shame that the murder could not have been anticipated and prevented since the character and reputation of the assassin was so well known. Shame that the deed was done in the courthouse and in the presence of officers and guardians of the law, at least two of whom were seen to dive under a table when the shooting started. Shame that the killer made his escape without the slightest attempt of anyone to apprehend him. The men who were present began to feel that they were under a tacit accusation of cowardice which they regarded terribly unjust in view of the facts. The slimy "If I'd a been there…." gossipers had a field day. The officials especially felt vulnerable to criticism and made heroic efforts to track Edgar down by way of atonement as well as determination to rid the area of a deadly menace hanging over it as long as Edgar was at large

George N. Morris, Edgar's father and Deputy Sheriff, was a tragic victim of the crime. Disgraced by the son whom he had tried to shield so many times, he resigned his post, a ruined man, but this was not the end of his sorrows.

There was no lack of explanations why the men folk seem to cut such a sorry figure.

"It all happened so fast that nobody had time to think what to do."

"Everybody was kind of paralyzed. Couldn't believe it."

"First thought was to help Son Sullivan."

"By the time folks had pulled themselves together, Edgar was gone."

"We had to look out for the women and the children."

47

"Of course we ducked. Wouldn't you if a pistol out of reach was pointing right at you?"

"We remembered Hillsville and the Allens and didn't want a gun fight where women and children would be killed."

The memory of Hillsville and the Allens was still a dreadful one. There was considerable merit to the defense. "We didn't want another Hillsville here."

For on March 14,1912, in the jammed courtroom in Hillsville, the seat of Carroll County in the mountains of southwestern Virginia, Floyd Allen, the head of a high spirited family, on trial for disturbing the peace, stood to hear the verdict of the jury, "Guilty as charged," followed by the sentence of the judge, "One year in the penitentiary." Floyd listened unbelievingly and looked around the room where many men of his tribe, all armed, stiffened and looked at their chief for some signal. There was an ominous silence and then Floyd spoke, "Gentlemen, I don't aim to go." Like a flash a gun battle broke out between the Allen clan and the officials of the county regardless of the fact that the courtroom was filled with men, women, and children of all ages. For a short span that seemed forever, there was indescribable chaos and then it was over. Dead were the Judge, the Commonwealth's Attorney, the Sheriff, two jurors, and a witness. The Clerk and several others were wounded. Months later Floyd Allen and his son, Claude, were electrocuted for their part in the crime, and other members of the so-called "Allen Gang" drew stiff jail sentences.

In Stanardsville, it was agreed, when matters cooled down, that the Edgar affair had all the makings of another such calamity, and gossip subsided for the nonce. Then one month after Justice Sullivan's death came word from Elkins, West Virginia that Edgar had been captured and was behind bars. The news when confirmed brought a vast sense of release from tension and fear. Details were vague but the story as it unfolded had a familiar sound.

On May 1 Sheriff Marstiller got a wire saying that Edgar Morris was in Elkins or was on the way there. Next he got a tip that Edgar was going to the Grand Restaurant that evening at about 8 o'clock. This fortunate development was doubtless due to the promise of a $1,000 reward to anyone furnishing information leading to Edgar's arrest. The Sheriff and his deputies laid a trap for him. Edgar entered the restaurant at the time the informer indicated. Almost immediately the Sheriff and his force followed him and took him by surprise. Even so, Edgar put up a desperate fight and he was reported to have drawn his revolver, but before he could level it at the Sheriff a deputy came up behind him and pinioned his arms.

That was the end of Edgar's freedom, and soon Sheriff Malone of Greene County and his deputies came for him and took him to the jail in Charlottesville for safe keeping because feelings were running high and many threats, more or less serious, were being made of an attempt to lynch him. Two brilliant lawyers were engaged to defend Edgar as the prosecution was going to ask for the death penalty, and the task of saving him from the electric chair was going to be most difficult. Since it was obvious that Edgar could not get a fair trial in Greene County, it was shifted to the Circuit Court of Albemarle at the behest of his attorneys, and the date was set for June 2. But the trial did not begin then. A host of witnesses had been summoned, but when court convened, most were missing. Some were reported sick with indefinite illnesses. Others were scattered to various points of the compass: Bath County, Augusta County, Warm Springs, West Virginia, and so on. June 23 was then set for the trial as it was virtually certain that the witness problem could be solved by that time. The trouble was that many of them did not want to be involved regardless of their personal feelings. The Morrises and the Sullivans had numbers of kin, and to appear to take sides could make enemies. Just getting on the witness stand would be bad enough.

But justice was not to be denied, and the trial got under way on the appointed day. The prosecution had an easy time presenting its case. Witness after witness told the same story. Justice Sullivan made no effort to harm Edgar. It was doubtful that Justice Sullivan even saw his killer before the first shot was fired. He was given no chance to defend himself. None of them had ever heard Justice Sullivan threaten to harm Edgar. All agreed that the victim was an honorable man, fearless in carrying out the duties of his office, highly respected, and was feared only by those who don't behave themselves.

On the other hand, witness after witness testified that Edgar on many occasions had threatened to kill the magistrate and had gone so far as to show the cartridges with which he expected to do the job "if Son

Sullivan kept bothering with my business." On cross examination, the defense lawyers not only failed to shake the witnesses for the prosecution but elicited additional damaging information.

When the turn of the defense came, some witnesses were called in an effort to damage the reputation of Justice Sullivan and show him as a bad tempered person feared by many, quick to draw his pistol and threaten those who crossed him and who especially had it in for Edgar. But this line was quickly abandoned when these witnesses folded under cross-examination. Then Edgar's lawyers unexpectedly put him on the stand. It became obvious that they had prepared well for this moment. Those who attended the first day of the trial noted a change in Edgar. He was an Edgar quite different from the image the public had of him. He did not look like the hot-tempered, cruel, stupid, bloodthirsty boor who gloried in making trouble. This Edgar was well dressed and groomed. He was self-possessed, quiet, courteous. His physique was impressive, and he looked almost handsome. The picture he presented was very pleasing, and one almost forgot that this fine looking young man was facing the chair, accused of having committed a despicable crime. As can be imagined, this new image did him no harm and may possibly have helped to save his life.

His justification for killing Justice Sullivan followed a very simple line. He had been threatened often by Son Sullivan, who was known to be quick with a pistol. Whenever he was near Sullivan, he feared for his life. On the day he did what he thought he had to do, he took his seat and looked around and saw that the Justice had a book in his hand and was reading from it until he saw Edgar. Then he quickly put it down and seemed to reach for his gun. Edgar said that he felt that he had to act fast to save himself. He used two guns so as to be sure to get Sullivan before Sullivan got him. He ran away because he couldn't bear to think of going to the pen. As Edgar talked, it became clear that his whole case rested on whether or not he could support his claim that his enemy "began to draw". This had already been denied by two justices, his own counsel in the trial which was pending when he slew Justice Sullivan, and by six citizens of excellent repute who were eye-witnesses. Later, Edgar's father would cast some doubt on his son's contention of self-defense. When Edgar's lawyers asked Edgar questions, he rambled and seemed to have trouble remembering details, so they switched to interrogating him about his childhood and youth.

In a soft voice, so soft that the judge had to request him to speak much louder, he said his mother died when he was born and he was raised by his grandfather who let him do pretty much as he pleased. His father was away from home much of the tine. He got no education. He couldn't catch on to figuring. He could write his name and read print some and that was all. While he spoke, the courtroom was very still and some seemed to be deeply moved and began to speak of Edgar as "that poor boy", which seemed to betoken some change in attitude toward Edgar.

Out in the city, a definite wave of sympathy began to swell. Years later, some of the Stanardsville people were still gossiping about these unhappy events. According to one informant, "The women. The women in Charlottesville, they had something to do with keeping Edgar out of the chair. They went wild over him. They visited him in jail and made over him. They brought him pies and cake. They plastered him with sympathy. They went around the city crying and blubbering, saying that it would be an everlasting shame to electrocute that pitiful young man who never had a decent chance to make something of himself. They got a lot of people to think like they did. Edgar owes a lot to those women." This informant may or may not have been correct in his opinion, but public opinion did seem to soften.

It took Edgar three hours to present his side, and he appeared to think that he had done well for himself, but under cross-examination he faltered badly, lost much of his composure and failed to support convincingly his contention that he saw Sullivan start to draw his gun.

When the prosecution presented its rebuttal, a very damaging piece of evidence was offered by the undertaker who handled the body of the dead magistrate. He examined his overcoat and found in the right hand pocket a 38 caliber pistol underneath a pair of heavy winter gloves, showing that Sullivan had made no effort to draw his gun. It was thought this testimony just about clinched the prosecution's case.

The trial dragged on a while longer, and soon opposing counsel were ready for the argument of the case. This produced much impassioned oratory but little else except an unexpected interruption of the proceedings. The leading counsel for the defendant reached a high peak of emotion and cried, "Bluford Sullivan was a man who feared neither man nor God." At this, the Episcopal minister, who was Justice Sullivan's pastor, stood up in the gallery and exclaimed angrily, "You are a liar." Immediately the judge ordered that the offender be brought to him and gave him a stern reprimand and fined the clergyman ten dollars.

Though this was a relatively minor matter, there were some who wondered if the jury might in some way have been negatively affected by it.

Finally the case was given to the jury, and tension began to rise as the jurymen departed to consider their verdict. Night came and there was surprisingly no verdict. The judge notified the jury that he would let them consider their findings in the case overnight and expressed the hope that this would allow them to render a verdict in the morning. They did, and Edgar was found guilty of murder in the second degree. The judge then sentenced Edgar to serve in the penitentiary eighteen years. Edgar seemed pleased and bowed to the jurymen. His lawyers were satisfied. No motion was made to set aside the verdict. The outcome angered some and pleased others, but all appeared happy that the long agony was over at last.

It was customary in those less sophisticated years to moralize a bit under such circumstances and to point to the silver lining, if any. True to form the reporter of the Charlottesville paper, the <u>Daily Progress</u>, wound up his story thus:

> "By good behavior the convicted youth—he is in his 22nd year—may return to his home within about 10 years on a conditional pardon, and begin life anew with clearer and better founded notions of the laws of his native State and of the rights and privileges of others.
>
> Who knows but that he may yet live to redeem his misguided youth and give his community long years of useful service and his sorrowing and afflicted family and friends cause for pride and gratification from the example his later years may be to others."

Chapter 6

HITCH HIKER HOMILIES

It was a gusty afternoon early in November of 1931. The leaves, which had clung tightly to their boughs, were now unloosening their grip with one accord and were deluging the browning earth with a flood of colors. There was a snap in the air, which made one's ears tingle. Grey clouds from the west were spreading over the sky, and there was a hint of an early snow.

I was driving along a winding mountain pike, which twisted through endless woods. The trees pressed in closely as though eager to overwhelm the narrow, rocky road and seemingly were held back only by the split rail fences zigzagging on both sides. By now the flying leaves had quite covered the ground and filled the drain ditches paralleling the highway. Though in a hurry to get home, I drove slowly for the car had already skidded a few times where the leaves were deep. Night was coming on, and an autumn glow was settling over the countryside.

Suddenly, I became aware of the form of a man lying face down in the ditch to the right and a few yards ahead. Startled and alarmed, I slammed on the brake. The machine stopped almost in an instant, throwing me forward against the steering wheel and causing a raucous blast from the horn.

At the sound, the prostrate figure came alive. His head jerked up, and a pair of surprised black eyes stared from under the brim of a battered black hat and over a bristling grey mustache. After a moment's unblinking gaze, he got up and walked stiffly over to the car. He appeared to be a man of over sixty, tall and thickset. He was wearing faded blue overalls and a tightly buttoned leather short coat. His feet were encased in a badly worn pair of galoshes. His hands clutched a trowel, a level and a short-handled mason's hammer.

"Be you going toward the courthouse?' he asked after studying me for a minute or two. I replied in the affirmative. Without more ado he opened the door and climbed in beside me. "Think I'll go along with you", he said, dropping his tools on the floor.

As I started up, he resumed looking at me intently. Presently "Ain't I seen you somewhars? Don't you live at the courthouse?"

"Yes," I responded.

"Been thar long?"

"About a year."

"Thought I knowed you. Thought I knowed you", he declared, nodding his head vigorously and blowing through his mustache, which I soon discovered was a nervous habit of his. There he let the conversation drop for a while and sat staring at the road.

"Who are you?" I questioned, thinking that some explanation was due from him.

Turning partly around, he stared at me with some bewilderment.

"Hunh? Don't you know me? Why, I'm old Jonas Knight. Yes sir, old Jonas Knight. That's who I am. You've heard tell of me, I know."

I was forced to admit that the name conveyed absolutely nothing to me. The old man slumped farther down into the seat, knit his brows and gazed at the road as though puzzling over the matter. Presently he sighed and turned to me.

"I'm Jonas Knight, the mason. I done most of the rock and brick work in this part of Virginia," he stated, waving his hand about vaguely. "Thar's lots of other masons 'round here, but I done forgot more'n they ever knew. Jonas Knight's work speaks for itself. I git all the work I can tend to. Everybody knows Jonas Knight and when they got a rock job, they call for me right away, 'cause my work speaks for itself. I live three miles this side the courthouse. Why, you must be more of a stranger in these parts than I thought if you ain't heard of old Jonas Knight!"

Again he contemplated the road ahead, blowing through his mustache the while. I felt that another matter needed clearing up.

"What were you doing lying in that ditch? Playing 'possum?"

"I was cold, mister, I was cold. Laid down thar to git out of the wind. The cold had done got to my bones. Been walking a right fur piece and was aiming for to git home tonight. But the cold got to my bones and I laid down thar for to warm up and to wait for a ride my way. Say, mister, ain't you got some likker with you, maybe?"

I replied in the negative. He sighed deeply and murmured, "Ain't that just too bad! Ain't nothing like a little nip to git the cold out of a man's bones this time of year. Nothing like it, sir, nothing like it."

"Are you on your way home now?" I asked to change the subject.

"Yes sir. Quit work this morning. Quit for the winter. I always quit come cold weather. It's hard to do rock work when my fingers git numb. Then too, cold gits to my bones and I can't stand it. Course, a little likker might help some, but when I drink enough to git the best of the cold, it's generally done got the best of me. No sir, when it gits cold, I git fur home. Won't work for nobody, come cold weather."

"Why, it doesn't seem cold enough to have to stop work outside", I objected. "Yes it is", affirmed my passenger, nodding his head vigorously. "You see, mud froze this morning and when mud freezes, I quit."

There had been no rain for two weeks in this section, hence there was no mud to freeze. I saw no connection anyway.

"Mud?" I repeated, puzzled.

Yes, mud. Mortar, you know. What you stick rocks together with. Only I calls it mud. When mud freezes it's no account and you can't do no good job, so I quit this morning."

"Oh! I understand now", I said. "You picked a bad day for a long walk home, didn't you?"

"Didn't think I was a-going to have to walk home", he replied. "Now here's the way it come about. Gyp Collins, he lives back thar a piece", he said, jerking his thumb over his shoulder. "You wouldn't know whar it is, being a stranger and all that. Anyway, Gyp comes to me a little over a week ago and says he wants me to put up a chimney for him in place of an old one he tore down last summer. Said he needed it before cold weather caught him. So I says, 'Gyp, you waited too long. Cold weather'll be here before I can git it up.' Yes sir, jest what I told him. But he kept after me and kept after me. Said he would pay me well and see I got a ride home. So I says, 'All right Gyp, but you waited too long, yes sir, too long.'

'Well, last night the chimney lacked 'bout four feet of being done. This morning when I fixed the first batch of mud, right off it began to freeze. So I leaned the hoe up 'side the house, got my tools together and says to Gyp, 'I'm a-quitting.' He says, 'What for?' I says, 'Mud's a-freezing!' 'Makes no difference', he says. 'I got to have that chimney done. You can't quit now!' 'Mud's a-freezing' I says. 'You and everybody knows I don't do no work when mud's a-freezing. I told you it was too late.'

"My, you ought to heard him rip and r'ar! He talked to me awful bad, he did. Now when folks talk to me like that, I don't stand for it, not for a minute. I always walk away. So I walked away this morning with him waving his arms and shouting like a crazy man. But I was mighty far from home and didn't git no money neither", he sighed.

"You see, mister", he said leaning toward me and speaking earnestly, "I know it looks bad to go off and leave a man in that fix but 'spose I had finished that thar chimney. It would have been a bad job with mud a-freezing. It wouldn't have hilt together and first thing you know the top of that chimney would begin to crack and come to pieces. And spose somebody, what wanted some brick work done, had come that way, he'd a-said, 'Gyp, who done that onery job for you?' And he'd a-said 'Old man Jonas Knight done it.' And he'd a-said, 'Humph! He'll never do no work fur me!'

"You see, I ain't like some folks. I don't brag on what I can do. I let my work speak for itself. If a man says to me, 'Jonas, can you do good work?' I only says, 'Go look at the wall I put up for Pap Evans. That's the kind of work I do.' My work talks better than I can. You see, when I finished a job, somewhars on it you can find my initials J.K. When you sees them, you know it's a good job." We drove on for a few minutes in silence. After puffing through his mustache a bit, my new found friend turned to me again.

"You know, you skeered me something terrible when you slipped up on me and blew your horn so loud. 'Course I'd been hoping for a ride, but I didn't hear you come up, the leaves being so deep and all. Folks git done lots of harm sometimes, mister, when they git a fright", he continued reprovingly. "I know what I'm talking about. Take my first wife. Martha her name was. You know, I been married three times. Yes sir, three times. She was the best cook I ever seen. When she fixed my vittles, I lived high. She sure knew how to cook up greens and hog jowl, and her biscuits would just melt in your mouth.

"Well, my oldest gal had growed up and married a man what owned a farm down near Richmond. One day Martha took a notion that she wanted to go down thar for a visit, 'cause she wanted to see the folks and since she hadn't been anywhars much outside the mountains. I didn't want her to go and leave me alone, her being such a good cook and all, but she went. You know how women is sometimes. It was the time of the State Fair,. and my gal took Martha to see it. Now that was all right, but what do you reckon she had to go and do then? She took her ma for a ride on that thar ferris wheel, she pointedly did. She ought to had better sense. She knowed her ma ain't never seen nothing like that and was bound to git skeered. They got on and started riding, they did. In no time at all, when they was plumb on top way up high, the thing stopped when something got out of kilter with the machinery. They sot thar mighty near an hour 'fore they got it fixed. My gal told me Martha only said, 'Gracious, how we going to git down now?' but she hilt on to her mighty tight. From then on Martha was a changed woman.

"When she come home, I says to myself, 'Something's wrong with Martha.' And believe me it was. She'd mope around, she would, and mumble to herself like. When she was doing the cooking, she would sit thar and let the vittles burn up. And from that day to the day she died, her biscuits wasn't worth a damn! No sir, they wasn't. 'Twas hard on me but it shows what gitting skeered will do to people.

"She was a good wife though. All three of my women has been all right. I got a good one now. I'm a good judge of women. I ought to be, being married three times. When I lost my second wife and was thinking of marrying again, they called me an old fool and said I'd see a hard time. I'm 'round sixty-five you see. But Sally's been a good wife. She's treated me right and I aim to treat her right. When a person treats me squar' and tells me the truth, I do right by them.

"Sally had never been to them talking pictures now. I never been neither—don't take no stock in 'em. But Sally wanted to go and I took her. Cost thirty-five cents apiece, those tickets did. I didn't mind that 'cause I treats them right what treats me right. So I took her to the pictures. Ain't been since. Don't take no stock in 'em. Sally's a good woman, so I like to do things for her, I do.

"Take last Christmas. I was fixing to go down to North Carolina. I had to see about some taxes whar I owned some land. It was Christmas and I wanted to do something for her. She'd been talking about wanting some overshoes, it being muddy and all. So I took her to the store. 'Let's see some overshoes,' I says to the man. He took down a few boxes and Sally tries on a pair. 'Does they fit?' I says. 'Yes', she says. 'Do you like 'em?' I asks. She says, 'Yes'. Then I tells her 'They're yours. I'm giving 'em to you for Christmas.' I give the man two dollars for 'em too. But I didn't mind that, 'cause Sally's treated me right, and I treats them right what treats me right.

"She'll be surprised to see me coming home so soon. Told her I'd be gone another week yet. I want to see how the baby's gitting on. When I left she was fretting, having a hard time cutting teeth and all. She wasn't a bit peart. As I was leaving, Sally asks if she must git a doctor, with the baby feeling so puny. I says, 'No, Jest you git a mole's toe and tie it 'round the gal's neck and it'll cure her in no time.' I got a letter yesterday and Sally said she fixed the toe and the baby seems tol'able peart now.

"You see, Mister, I don't take no stock in doctors. I'm going on sixty-five, maybe sixty-six, and I never called but one doctor in my life. They jest wants the money. The Lord put you here and he's going to take you away when He gits good and ready. When your time comes, can't no doctor—nor no hospital neither—stop your going. What's a hospital good for? Jest to be born in and to die in, that's all. When I gits flat on my back, I trusts in the Lord. He can do more for me in a minute than all the doctors in a year. It's this a-way: the doctors takes the money but the Lord does the curing!"

Jonas Knight paused in his harangue and scowled ferociously at some small boys beside the road who were throwing acorns at the car as we passed.

"Don't know what children are coming to these days. They gits worser and worser", he growled. "When I was a boy, parents raised their children. But now children are raising their parents. Children are so bad that they don't pay no attention to what the old folks tell 'em, but tells the old folks what to do. Yes sir, I seen it many times. Now boys and gals go riding 'round in cars 'stead of staying home and learning what they can. They don't want nothing but a good time like going to the moving pictures. (Took Sally to 'em once but ain't been since. Don't take no stock in 'em) Children go to 'em and pay thirty-five cents a ticket, they does. If they ever go to church, they won't put over a nickel in the plate to save 'em. Done seen it many a time. They don't know nothing but act like they know it all. Does beat all what things are coming to. Now to tell you the truth, mister, it jest don't look like nothin's been right since the Republicans got holt of this country the last ten years. 'Deed it don't.

"Now, mister, I always been a Democrat and always will. The Republicans are the ruination of this country like the old folks tell 'bout after Marse Robert surrendered. Vote for a Republican and you're jest voting for destruction. I've voted for a Democrat every time 'cept the last one."

"Oh! So you are one of those good Democrats who helped make Virginia go for Mr. Hoover?" I accused him.

"Who? Me! I did not. He's a Republican and I don't vote for no Republican, no time!"

"Well, why didn't you vote for Al Smith?"

"I'll tell you," said my passenger after a pause, "It warn't 'cause of his religion that I didn't vote for him. Thar's the commonwealth lawyer what said to me one day we hadn't ought to vote for Al Smith 'cause he's a Catholic. He says so to me right in front of the Post Office. Now, I'll tell you jest like I told him, that it ain't right to hold a man's religion against him. It's his business and it ain't our'n. And for that matter, thar ain't no reason why a Catholic can't make as good a president as a Baptist or a Methodist, or a better one even.

"But one of the magistrates, who is a right smart politician, he got hold of me one court day and says to me, 'Don't you vote for Al Smith 'cause if he's elected, he'll put us under a king and a queen.' Now you know, mister, that we was under a king and a queen once and we had to fight 'em. Yes sir, we pintedly did. Now, I didn't mind Al Smith's being a Catholic, but jest couldn't stand for that king and queen business. So I didn't vote for nobody,"

Again, my companion fell silent and stared at the roadway. Just ahead, at the top of a steep rise, there loomed a barnlike structure on the right of the road. A hideous squat steeple marked it as another of those ugly, austere places of worship so characteristic of certain sections of rural Virginia.

"Colored church", commented my garrulous hitchhiker, jerking his thumb toward the now receding building. "Used to be a white folk's church but they sold it to the black folks for $400 and built somewhars else. It's got five hundred members, they tells me, and, man sir, they has big meetings, 'specially in the summer time. Now and then I like to go to colored preaching. Some white folks go jest to see 'em shout, and moan, and fall out. I don't think that's right, I don't. It's all mighty serious to them, and a white person ain't got no call to poke fun at their religion. I like their music. They sure can sing. Beat the white folks any day. Any day, sir.

"I had to laugh at one preacher though, and do every time I think of him. He had been exhorting till he got himself all worked up and was a-sweating like he'd been hoeing corn under a hot sun all day. He stopped shouting for a minute, he did, and looked up at the ceiling of the church. Then he hilt up his arms and says, trancelike, 'O Lord, come down! Come down, 'mongst us sinners here! Come through the roof! Come right through the shingles, and I'll pay for every one you bust off!'

"I don't belong to no church. I drinks, you see, so I don't feel right 'bout joining up. Preachers keep gitting after me. They tells me I'm a-gitting old and that my chances are gitting slimmer every day. They say I better let 'em baptize me so I can git clean. But I tell you, mister, like I tell them, 'tain't none of the preachers what can do nothing 'bout me and my sins. That's betwixt me and the Lord. No preacher can save me. Me and the Lord's going to work that out. Before I can git clean outside, I must git clean inside. 'Tain't none of the preachers living that can do that. That's what I tell 'em, yes sir. I don't care if they tell me I'm a-going to hell for not joining up.

"Oh, I goes to church. I go near 'bout every Sunday. I like to hear good preaching, I do, and I'll listen long's I agree with the preacher. If he says something I don't like, I don't listen. I never did walk out on but one preacher though.

"It was when they was a-burying John Harris' baby. That was 'bout twenty years ago. It was summer and it was mighty hot. I know 'cause I went to the burying. Thar was a big crowd standing 'round in the yard.

It was mighty hot. I was thar standing by the front gate with Jeems Scott. The coffin was on the front porch, and the baby was in it. A gal she was, 'bout two years old. A preacher was thar to preach the funeral, and he was standing back of the little coffin.

"Thar stood the preacher and the yard was full of people. He stood thar preaching he did, and he said 'Folks, thar's babies in hell not a span long.' That's what he said, yes sir, 'Babies in hell not a span long', and he hilt up his hand to measure. I seen him and I heard him say it, 'cause I was thar, standing by the gate with Jeems Scott. I couldn't stand for that, so I says to Jeems:

" 'Jeems, you got any likker in the still house?' He was running a still in those days, had a license for it from the government.

" 'Plenty', he says.

" 'Well, I want two pints', I says. 'If thar's babies in hell not a span long, what chance is thar for me, nor for you, nor for that preacher? If that is so, I might as well drink all I want, for what chance have I got?

"So 1 walked away with Jeems Scott. I couldn't stand for no such talk. I don't believe the Lord puts babies in hell. I believe that thar poor baby girl has her resting place—and all babies too—and it ain't in hell neither. When I heard that man stand over that coffin and preach that baby to hell, I couldn't stand it. So I went and got drunk. I pintedly did!"

After this outburst, he fell silent. By this time we were not so very far from the county seat, and I was wondering where my passenger lived. As though anticipating my question, he straightened up.

"I live jest beyond this turn, mister. Whoa-up! Here's whar I live", he said as we rounded the bend and came abreast of a dilapidated one-story frame building, sitting a few yards from the road in a bare but clean clearing. As I stopped, a hound, chained to a post near the door-step, set up a furious barking. A stout woman, with a crying baby in her arms, came to the door and stared.

"Git out and come in won't you?" invited my companion, as he gathered up his tools and got out of the car. "Be mighty glad to have you for supper. Can't come in? Too bad! Well, come to see us sometime. Bring your wife and stay all day. You're welcome any time."

With a friendly wave, he turned and strode up the walk to the house where the woman, with an expression of mild surprise, awaited her returning lord.

Chapter 7

A PROMISE AND A SLIP

Jonas Knight, after our first meeting, became a very close and interesting friend as time went by. Before I came to the field, he had helped with the building of two of our mission churches and liked to attend services at them when possible. He paid little attention to what went on but spent the time looking around at the walls, admiring his handiwork of which he was inordinately proud. He enjoyed visiting other churches too because he had many friends in the county, and this gave him a chance to meet and chat with them.

Knowing this, after our acquaintance ripened, I frequently stopped by his place and took him along on the Sundays when I was scheduled to hold services at these distant missions. I had a special reason for doing so. Jonas' weekends were usually lost weekends because he had an alcoholic problem, and I thought that if I could give him an outing, he would have a reasonably sober Sunday. Sometimes it worked and sometimes it didn't. This posed a dilemma for me. If I got him before he started drinking, he would be a staid and rather dull companion. On the other hand, if he had gotten a good start before my arrival, he would be in a glow and our trip would be most interesting.

On these occasions, Jonas was almost a non-stop talker, relegating me wholly to the position of a listener. When he asked questions, I soon discovered that they were purely rhetorical, because he seldom waited for an answer, and his occasional pauses served only to allow him to catch his breath before rushing on to the next topic. His fund of information was astounding and covered a wide range, even though he insisted that he was an ignorant man due to the fact that his folks were left so poor "after the war" that he had to forget about schooling and learn a trade if he wanted to eat.

"After the war" referred to the Civil War, for memories of it were still vivid in spite of the passage of time. Jonas spoke of it as though it were yesterday and as though he had been an eye-witness of many of its tragic events. I was surprised by some of the footnotes that he appended to Civil War history which were quite new to me. I challenged him often as to the accuracy and source of his information.

"Where did you hear all this?" I asked him the first time.

"From the old folks, of course," he replied somewhat miffed. "From the old folks what was thar and seen it. You can't do no better than that! You sure can't! Most of what I knows I got from the old folks and not from books. You can't always be sure about what you find in books. I don't do much reading. I kin read if I have a mind to, but I ain't got a book in my house 'cept maybe the Bible. I got most of my l'arning from listening to the folks what knew things. That's the best kind.

"You see, Mr. Preacher, my pa fit in the Confederate army most of the war, he did. Pa said Stonewall Jackson was a fine general but he fit his men too hard. More men died from marching and camping in the cold and wet and snow than they did from bullets. Pa said so many a time, and I heard him. Jackson was always short of men 'cause so many fell out from being walked to death. So one time when he was a-fighting up and down the Valley, he sent some soldiers up in the mountains, not so fur from here, to round up conscripts but they didn't stay long, no sir! They tell me those mountain boys got their guns and formed a line of battle good as any general and ran those soldiers out. And they didn't come back, neither!

"When I was a boy, thar was three or four old veterans in the country 'round whar I growed up. They and my pa used to git together sometimes and talk 'bout the war. I hung round and listened to their tales and heard more than you will ever l'arn in school. One old soldier liked to talk 'bout the time when we whupped old Burnside and drove the Yankees back over the river at Fredericksburg—leastways what was left. He was in the artillery and was up in the hills above the town and seen the Yankees a-coming, but they was ready for 'em. He and his men was firing canister—it's a sight to behold! They shot down the Yankees as fast as they come 'til they quit charging and laid down on the ground. Thar they stayed all the night and all the next day—nobody could figure out why. Didn't make no sense! Many a bluecoat died from wounds or froze to death. Sharpshooters killed a lot 'cause soldiers just couldn't lie still all day. Come morning, they was all gone—the live ones, I mean.

"This old fellow said Marse Robert's men couldn't figure out what "made those Yankees fight so crazy 'til they got back down into Fredericksburg after old Burnside was gone. The place was a mess—all tore up and the houses that wasn't burned was looted. They found a few folks what couldn't git away before the shooting started. Some had tales to tell, like before the Yankee officers lined up their men along the streets for to fight up the hills, barrels of likker was rolled out of wagons and stood up along the way they was setting out on to tackle General Lee.

"Yes sir! That's what they said—rolled out more likker than you'll ever see. Then the heads of the barrels was busted in with axes and ready for the soldiers as they marched by. They took their tin cups and scooped up as much as they wanted to drink. Our boys claimed that Burnside's men had got roaring drunk by the time they got to the firing line and didn't care what they was doing. Seems like the folks up north said it was all a lie, but the old man what told the tale said he didn't pay no attention to what the Yankees said 'cause he was thar and heard it from the folks what saw it all.

"Then I mind another veteran what was with Jubal Early the last of the war before the Yankees finished him and his army off in the Valley. He had something to tell what you won't find in the history books, so 'taint no use looking. One night, he and my pa was talking 'bout the old days when they got onto old Jubal Early and the time he could have took Washington and didn't. General Early took his army into Maryland and whupped some Yankee General. Thar was then nobody between him and Abe Lincoln what could have stopped him. All he had to do was to walk in to the White House and say howdy! General Early always claimed he didn't do it 'cause he didn't know what to do with the place if he had it. Anyways, he said General Lee told him to keep moving around and worry the Yankees. So, he backtracked across the Potomac.

65

"But that ain't the way I heard it. This old soldier I was talking 'bout pintedly said Jubal Early didn't take Washington 'cause he was lying dead drunk in a ambulance until too late. He said he himself walked by the ambulance and seen him thar all wrapped up in a linen duster. He said plenty more seen him lying thar too and could tell it like he did if they wanted to. You see, Mr. Preacher, thar's a heap of things what never gits told."

"Now wait a minute, Mr. Jonas," I cut in. "I have read a lot about the Civil War. I have many books on the subject which I have studied carefully and I never ran across this tale."

Jonas stared at me pityingly and blew through his mustache a time or two pondering my stupidity. Then he tapped my knee and said earnestly, "Don't let that worry you none, Mr. Preacher. You're a educated man. You know as well as me that a thing don't have to be writ down to be true. And, you know mighty well that not everything writ down is true. I don't trust all what is writ down nohow. I put my dependence in them what sees things and knows things; them what has been thar. When it comes to writing, it depends on who's doing the writing and what he's writing for, and what he's got on his mind. Now, 'bout history in these parts I kin tell you a heap more."

And he did.

From him also I got an insight into the local political lineups that were so often the source of feuds and even out-breaks of violence, of the social patterns, and of the family groups which did not "hold" with other family groups, especially if mountain ridges separated them. He pointed out the areas where I could travel without care and those where I might be viewed with suspicion. Jonas seemed to have a rather wide acquaintance with bootleggers, and, though he avoided using names, he talked freely of their operations, their problems and mischances.

Since he had patronized them for years, he was eminently qualified to do so. As an illustration, he related the remarkable adventure of one of them and referred to him simply as "Tom". "You wouldn't know him nohow," he explained.

It so happened that one day Tom became a bit nervous when he got word that Federal officers were combing the hills near his place. He had his still and his mash barrels hidden very carefully, but he double-checked to be sure. However, his mind was not at ease because the "guv'ment folks" were getting hard to fool. Thinking it over, Tom decided that he needed to take out more insurance. Before long he would be ready for a "run". A raid right now would ruin his business, not to mention the risk of prison.

So Tom saddled up his horse, rode over the ridge and down to Port Republic to find a "conjur" woman of whom he had heard very favorable reports. It didn't take long to find her, since she had quite a reputation in those parts. After dickering for a while, she agreed to put a spell on him for twenty-five dollars. When Tom demurred at the price, she claimed that the spell was a strong one and would surely protect him from the law. She allowed that if it didn't work, he could get his money back. So he paid her, and she wove the spell.

Once back home, Tom felt like a new man with no worries now. However, he had one big fault. He could not keep his mouth shut and began to brag to some friends about his investment. To his disgust, they ridiculed him unmercifully for believing such trash and throwing his money away like that. Worse yet, these friends told their wives about it, and they could not keep the secret. The affair stirred up quite a bit of gossip, and some of it reached the ears of the authorities.

In almost no time at all, Federal officers descended on Tom's farm. But for some inexplicable reason, they failed to locate the still and the mash, even though they gave the premises a thorough overhaul. After three hours, they not only left the place but they left Tom a nervous wreck and he began to wonder who had informed on him. In due time, he recovered from the scare and his suspicions of betrayal, convinced that he had spent his money wisely and that magic charms were grossly underrated. Also, his bewildered cronies looked on him with new respect.

From time to time, Jonas and I got on the subject of religion and of church membership. He confided that he had never been baptized, even though "lots of preachers had done worked on me". Some time later, on the same subject, he stated that he wanted to join a church but couldn't.

"You see," he confessed, "I gits drunk and don't feel right 'bout it before the Lord. Now, I been studying some more 'bout it, and I'm sort of thinking of joining your church. But I got to git straight 'bout my drinking first. I'll tell you when I'm ready."

So there we left it. In fact, I had forgotten about the matter, when one Sunday months later I picked him up for another of our journeys. After we started off, I noticed that he was unusually quiet but I did not comment. After a while, he turned to me suddenly and said, "I'm ready!"

Caught by surprise, I asked, "Ready for what, Mr. Jonas?"

"Like I told you," he replied, "ready to join the church. I ain't had a drink for over six months and I feel right about it now."

To make a long story short, after suitable instruction, he was baptized and presented to the Bishop for confirmation. But prior to that, I discussed his problem with him frankly.

"Mr. Jonas, you have been a hard drinking man for most of your life. I am not going to ask you to promise never to take another drink. I don't think that would be wise, but I'm going to ask you to promise that you will not go on any more of your sprees which have made life so miserable for you and your family."

"I think that's real fa'r, I pintedlv do. I agrees to that, I sure do," he replied.

For almost a year, Jonas walked a straight line, contrary to the glum predictions of those who knew him well. However, one court day, some of his old cronies led him behind the jail house and produced a bottle of whiskey. It was too much for Jonas, and resolution wilted at the first sniff.

Some time later, an employee of the local bank was hard at work going over accounts. Suddenly, he heard a screech of brakes outside and angry shouts mingled with curses. Something was wrong out on the highway. He rushed to see what the trouble was and beheld a growing traffic jam nearing a state of chaos. On court day, everybody who could came into the little town, and traffic was worse than usual, and the cause of it all was Jonas. There he was in the middle of the road, oblivious to the traffic and everything else, weaving his way along and creating pandemonium. A bit more, the sheriff would appear and lock him up.

The banker, anguished to the depths of his prohibitionist soul at the sight, pushed his way through the chaos and pulled Jonas to the safety of the sidewalk. He propped him against the wall of the bank and proceeded to give him a tongue lashing. "Shame on you, Jonas! Here you are hog drunk in public for everybody to see. It's a scandal, especially since you joined the church such a little time ago! Backsliding already! What are people going to think of you? What is your minister going to think of you?"

With an airy wave of the hand, Jonas brushed aside all criticism, saying, "Now look a here, you sound just like my wife! Don't you worry none about me. Me and my preacher done had a heart to heart talk 'bout my drinking. He said to me right out and plain, Jonas, I don't want you to git drunk no more, but I don't care if you have a dram!"

I shall only add that I did not live that episode down as long as I lived in the county.

I must confess that Jonas quoted me correctly. (A "dram", by the way, is a very small amount of an alcoholic drink.) However, I have learned from this and many other hard experiences over the years that a true alcoholic should not have even a dram, because it is too difficult for him (or her) to stop with just one.

Chapter 8

WHO SHALL MY KEEPER BE?

The year 1930 found me once more in the mountains. Much had happened since my last stay. I had finished my Seminary course, had been ordained to the priesthood, and married my wife, Constance. Then followed a two year missionary tour in Brazil, which was cut short by tuberculosis. The chances of a cure in Brazil were not promising, so on the best medical advice, my wife and I returned to the United States, with our recently born daughter, Margaret. After a few months in a sanitarium, my specialist informed me that my recovery had been excellent and that I could start working again, provided that I avoided over-exhaustion and over-exposure. Since I was "damaged goods", there was no great demand for my services, but before long there was a vacancy in the mountain mission area, where I had worked previously, and the church authorities were willing to take a chance on me.

Thus, I found myself and my little family settled in a cure with six missions scattered over a difficult terrain and connected by very poor roads. Perhaps it was thought that a "kill or cure" job was best for all concerned. Anyway, there was nothing else, and in those dreadful early days of the Great Depression, any salary was a godsend and no one could be choosy, especially when the position included a rectory situated on thirteen acres of land, much of which became a source for all kinds of food—vegetables, chickens, ducks, geese, squabs, and milk—for five years.

Not long after we had settled down, I was sent word that Floyd Draper was in jail, charged with murder and was most anxious for me to visit him. The message both pleased and distressed me. It had been six years since I first got to know the Draper family at the time when Floyd's older brother, Dave, had been shot and killed in what was called a "gredge fight". There were no witnesses besides the accused, who was given three years in the penitentiary on general principles. Under the emotional strain of Dave's death, the trial, and the verdict, which seemed trivial to Dave's family, Pat Draper, the father of these two men, suffered a stroke, which made an invalid of him for many months. I visited him often during his convalescence and so developed an affectionate relationship with the family and their kin.

So, tidings of new trouble for these people was depressing, as it seemed to me that they had suffered more than their share of grief. At the same time, I was glad to have the chance to see Floyd once more. I not only liked him very much, but I shall ever be grateful to him for saving me from being treed by a pair of mean, green-eyed dogs, which took a dislike to me one day when I was on foot in Scrougeabout Hollow, paying a few calls on the more or less faithful members of the mission.

Having just finished lunch when the message arrived, I walked to the courthouse square to pay the requested visit. On the way, I pondered what I could say to him by way of sympathy and encouragement under the circumstances. Not least of the circumstances was the fact that the jail of this poor county was a dark, smelly, vermin infested building. To think of Floyd locked up in one of the miserable cells made the bright April day seem a bit gloomy.

My pity was wasted. Coming up to the jail from the rear, I made my way around a noisome refuse dump, turned the corner, and there was Floyd seated in a split-bottom chair, leaning back against the outer brick wall of the jail, right beside the open entrance. The prisoner was whistling and whittling on a stick. He did not seem to have a care in the world. Not a single representative of law enforcement was in sight anywhere.

I was surprised but need not have been, because the sheriff kept his prisoners on a loose leash held by a firm hand. He avoided confining his wards as much as possible, and often took them out to work on his farms to give them exercise and plenty of time in the open air. This was a practice that subjected the sheriff to considerable criticism from certain public officials and social workers, who accused him of exploiting his charges for his personal gain. But this troubled him not in the slightest. His stock answer was, "Got to keep 'em busy to keep 'em out of trouble. 'Tain't human to keep 'em locked up in that sorry jail, 'less I have to". In general, he considered keeping his prisoners around the jail the same as keeping them in jail just as long as they did not wander too far and kept out of trouble. Once in a while, someone might take a notion to take to the hills. When this happened, such was the power and reputation of the sheriff that all he had to do was to send word that the ingrate had better show up the next day if he knew what was good for him. Seldom did he have to go out and chase the "dodger" down.

As soon as Floyd spied me, he jumped up and gave me a flattering welcome, declaring that he knew in his bones that I would not be long in coming around. Then, he darted into the jail, brought out another chair, and invited me to "set a spell". When we were settled, the first thing I noticed about him was an ugly scar starting at the right corner of his mouth, running along the jawbone, then under the ear and down the back of the neck where it disappeared behind his shirt collar. Even with close friends in the mountains, it is not wise to be directly inquisitive about personal affairs. Nor is it wise to ignore obvious troubles, lest one be thought to be lacking in fellow-feeling and compassion. Such matters are best approached obliquely. So, we spent some time in talk about the health of our respective families, the weather, crop prospects, and whether or not the "guvmint" was really going to run folks off their land and take it for the National Park.

Noting my surreptitious glances at his disfigurement, far from being offended, Floyd soon showed eagerness to tell me all about it. First, he took off his shirt (there was no undershirt) to show me the extent of the injury which was appalling, for the scar continued over the left shoulder blade and down to the belt line. He stated that he lost "right smart blood" and had to be driven fast to the University of Virginia Hospital, where it took fifty stitches to sew him up.

"And that", he affirmed, "was why I had to kill a man and that is why I'm here in this jail. I had to kill him, or I'd been dead: I had no choice!"

Pulling myself together a bit, I commented tritely, "It must have been a bad business to end in one man dead and you half dead!"

"You sure are right about that preacher!" he replied. "You and me are good friends, so 1 don't mind telling you my side. The good Lord knows that I got to tell it in court soon enough now. This fellow, what I killed, you wouldn't know him, had been caught for making and selling likker and was out on bail. He got it in his head for some reason that I had informed on him. As the Lord is my Judge, I had nothing to do with it. He talked around mighty bad about me and sent me word that if he ketched up with me, I better be ready to fight, because he was going to git even with me if it was the last thing he did, which it was. Truth is, I thought so little of him that I had no time to talk about him, much less to give him a bad name. He was a sorry sort of fellow, and his likker wasn't fit to drink, it was so dirty."

"What do you mean by dirty whiskey?" I asked.

"I mean he made it nasty. He didn't take no trouble to keep his mash clean when he buried his barrels out in the woods. He didn't have decent tops fur them. He put boards over them any old way and covered them with bresh. All kinds of things fell in his mash—toads, snakes, scarapins...."

"What in the world are scarapins?" I asked.

"You know, those little critters with long tails you see scooting along rock fences and across the road", he explained.

"Oh you mean lizards", I suggested.

"Maybe so, maybe so. Folks around here always call 'em scarapins. Anyway, they git into the mash if you ain't careful; chickens and 'possums too. Well, this fellow, he didn't care and he boiled the whole mess up when time came to make a run. He sold dirty likker to city folks who bragged on how good it was. It was just as well they didn't know what was in it. Well, I tried to keep out of this fellow's way, because I didn't aim to have no trouble. But I couldn't stay home all the time because of him. So, whenever I left home, I put a loaded pistol in my shirt just in case I come up on him sometime. That's why they are trying to say that I was set on killing him. It ain't so. I just couldn't take no chances.

"One day he comes across me down at the store near home and says for me to git ready, because I got to fight him. I asks him if he wants to fight fa'r or not fa'r. He agreed to fight fa'r. But I had no business to trust him. I knowed him for the low down fellow he was. After we grappled a time or two, I was gitting the best of him. Pulling loose from me, he

73

slipped and fell. Then he jumped up and come tearing at me again. I didn't see the knife he had in his right hand as he grabbed me. He held me tight with his left arm and gits his right hand clear back of me and starts cutting. Knowing I was in a bad way, I twisted jest enough to git my pistol out. I jammed it into his body, started pulling the trigger and kept on 'til he fell. I didn't know much after that because I was hurt bad and didn't care. The doctors told me that if I hadn't been in the good shape I was, I wouldn't have made it. They treated me wonderful at the hospital, but as soon as I could be moved, they brought me here, and I ain't worrying too much. It was self defense, plain as day. I don't think they'll have me sent away."

Shortly after Floyd finished stating his case to me, a car turned into the dusty road leading to the jail and pulled up with a jerk in front of the building. It was easy to recognize the four door "Tin Lizzie" of the Federal officer who was driving. Beside him in the front sat a stout, surly looking man, who was handcuffed. The back of the car seemed to be filled with a collection of metal junk. The officer, obviously in a bad mood, got out and came around to the other side of the car. He yanked the door open, jerked the prisoner from the seat, grabbed him by the coat collar and by the seat of his pants, rushed him into the jail, and literally threw him into a cell, locking the door after him.

Coming out again, the officer unloaded the flivver, piling in a corner of the jail yard the scrambled remains of a rather sizeable still. Then, he went back into the jail and came out with an axe, with which he made a thorough wreck of the contraption. He chopped the "worm" into three parts. I confiscated the spout piece of the "worm" as a suitable souvenir of the occasion and of my mountain sojourn. It now reposes on my living room table and makes a wonderful conversation piece. It is surprising how few people have even heard of a "worm".

Now for the unbelievable part of the tale. As the officer prepared to leave, he said to Floyd:

"That's a bad man I just locked up in there. He gave me an awful lot of trouble, and I had to handcuff him to bring him in. Now I want you to keep your eye on him and don't get too close to the bars when you give him water or something. No telling what he might do if he is not watched. I'm depending on you."

So saying, he got back into his car and took off in a cloud of dust, leaving me staring after him somewhat bewildered. Somehow it didn't seem real. Setting an accused killer to watch over a moonshiner seems to obliterate distinctions between crimes and to shake the ground of judgment. But those were the fantastic and delirious days of Prohibition—THE NOBLE EXPERIMENT—when anything could happen and usually did. At that time, the crime of crimes, before which all other forms of turpitude seemed to pale, was the illicit manufacture and sale of alcoholic beverages—mainly whiskey.

Sequel: In due time, Floyd was tried for murder. It was commonly assumed that the trial would be a mere formality and that he would be set free promptly. But to the shocked surprise of almost everyone, Floyd was sentenced to three years in the penitentiary, in spite of the evidence dramatically supporting the claim of self-defense.

Later on, the foreman of the jury explained to me the reasoning leading to the unexpected verdict:

"Sure it was self-defense. That scar left no argument when Floyd was stood up in court and stripped to the waist for all to see. What bothered us was that both of those boys were looking for a fight and both were guilty no matter who got hurt or killed. There didn't have to be a fight. We figured they were hunting each other. Floyd admitted that he carried a loaded pistol because he expected trouble and those that look for trouble usually find it. You know, as well as I do, that there is too much fighting and killing in these parts. Too many hot heads have been getting off by claiming self-defense. These young bucks have got to be taught a lesson. In Floyd's case, there didn't have to be a killing as we saw it. So we decided to send him away for a while to see if it wouldn't put a stop to such doings around here."

Chapter 9

PREACHERS ARE NOT ALWAYS WELCOME

Many casual visitors to Appalachia report that the people are hostile toward strangers. This is an exaggeration growing out of superficial observation and experience. True it is that the mountaineer is quite reserved, if not withdrawn, when first meeting outsiders. He answers questions briefly, volunteers no information, and is difficult to draw into conversation. He is not unfriendly. Basically, he is afraid, though he would die before admitting it.

In the first place, he does not know who the stranger is, nor why he has come up into the hill country. Is the "foreigner" an officer of the law? If so, that usually means big trouble for somebody among his kin and neighbors. Is the alien a social worker of some kind? Then there is going to be prying into someone's private affairs which are nobody else's business. Such have been known to come up and take away a man's children. Is the stranger selling something or looking for grazing land to buy up cheap? The hill folk have indelible memories of many of their kin having been swindled by fast-talking, sweet-talking men from "out yonder somewhars". Is the visitor looking around out of curiosity? In that case one had better have as little to do with such a person as possible. Chances are that he is going back to where he came from and make fun of the mountain folk, or maybe he is going to put a piece in the paper and give them a "bad name".

In addition, the mountaineer feels at a hopeless psychological disadvantage when he meets an outsider. He finds the differences between the two unnerving. The one has had little chance for a decent education; the other is obviously well schooled. The speech of one is unrefined, interlarded with archaic expressions; the other employs a vocabulary which at times is almost incomprehensible to the mountain man. The clothes of the one are coarse and plain; the clothes of the other are superior in quality and style. The manners of the one are rustic; the other is more assured and polished in meeting people.

This situation is difficult for a proud people to manage, for they acknowledge no superiors, but feel inferior by their own comparison. One thing they cannot endure is ridicule and humiliation, so they become defensive and tend to be reticent in the presence of strangers, who in turn too hastily describe the mountaineer as hostile, backward, and stupid.

It takes patience to win the friendship of these men and women, who are slow in committing themselves. For them two questions have to be answered, "Does that foreigner respect me and can I trust him?" Once this defensive reserve is broken through, one finds a warm response and good friends whose philosophy can be summed up as, "Do as I would be done by". Strong as the mountain man's friendship may become, it can change to bitter enmity when betrayed, for his pride is his most vulnerable spot.

All this I learned the hard way when I first came to work among them. It was a surprise to a novice to discover that good will was not enough and that acceptance was given only after a period of aloof observation. No small part of the task was to learn their way of talking and how to speak to them in their own terms without seeming "to talk down to them". But, even when accepted, one could not be sure that he was on firm ground.

There seemed to be in all the mountain folk a congenital undercurrent of suspicion—the being on guard when dealing with "people who are not like us". Outsiders were often dismayed when they discovered that they did not have the full confidence of the hill people whom they fondly thought had given them their complete trust. Mission workers, particularly, were not seldom shaken when acceptance suddenly and for reasons unknown changed to distrust and even to hostility, just as I was on one occasion when I attempted to organize mission work more efficiently with the help of another worker, Constance, who in due time became my wife.

Sunday School attendance at the chapel, which was located in a hollow known as Haneytown, was very spotty and, being the novices that we were, we decided to take a census of the children in the area and to make a record of their names and ages, so that we would know what the prospects were for building up the classes. Suddenly, a very friendly people froze, refused information, and some were scarcely even willing to speak to us. Our project ended then and there, and we were bewildered by the unforeseen change. In time, we found out what had happened when the freeze thawed.

Our attempt to list the children by name and age started a rumor, which ran like wild fire, that we were planning to take them away from their parents. The worst blow was to learn that the friendliest and most intelligent of the men and women had been going around the community saying of us, "Them folks ain't over here altogether for good". It all blew over when the people finally understood what we had in mind, but they vetoed adamantly any proposal to go on with the census. Some even called to mind how, according to the Bible, King David got into bad trouble when he undertook to number his subjects.

There was one special mountain family in whose home I could find a cordial welcome—that of Pat Draper. Our relationship began shortly after I first came into the mountain field at a time of tragedy for them. Two months before, Mr. Pat's oldest son, Dave, was shot and killed. Nearing twenty-one, he was handsome and undisciplined, and had given his parents much anxiety with his heavy drinking and his all too quick readiness to quarrel and to fight. When sober, he was charming, but when drunk, he could be exceedingly noisy and offensive. As a result, Dave had many enemies, especially among the young men of the county.

There were differing accounts of the killing, and gossip was rife due to the scarcity of witnesses. According to his family, Dave was sleeping beside the main road that afternoon when three youths, "who had a gredge against him", found him. One of them shook him awake and before Dave could defend himself, he was fatally shot. I tried to learn the source of their information, but their reply was, "Everybody knows it". Others, however, said that on awaking, Dave attacked the one who killed him and was shot in self-defense. I made no effort to ascertain the true facts because it was really none of my business as an outsider. Several families were involved, and it was well to avoid the appearance of taking sides.

The trial was held before the circuit court of Greene County a month later, during a spell of very hot weather. The affair attracted wide interest. The courthouse was packed, and, with poor ventilation, the heat was almost unbearable. The accused pleaded self-defense, and he was strongly supported by his companions. In spite of that, the jury did find the defendant guilty, and he was sentenced to three years in the penitentiary.

The seemingly light sentence outraged the Draper family and their friends who considered it trivial in view of the nature of the crime as they saw it—the malicious gunning down of a defenseless man. However, unusual verdicts like this were not uncommon. In a similar case three years before, the accused was acquitted on the grounds of self-defense but was fined ten dollars for carrying a pistol without a license.

Pat, greatly angered and already badly affected by the heat and emotional strain of the trial, suffered a stroke from which he recovered slowly. Hearing that a preacher had come to stay for a while at the Blue Ridge Industrial School, he sent word to me by a neighbor, "Please come to see me and preach me a sermon, 'cause I'm real sick and might not be here for long." Thus began a series of visits by me to the Draper home to ease their bitterness and distress as well as I could. During the summer, Pat made fair progress, with ups and downs, until he reached a point where he could get outdoors and do a few minor chores around his rocky farm. His family kept a close watch on him which really pleased him though he complained that he was being treated like a baby and would never get well at that rate.

The summer wore along and the time was approaching when I would have to leave the Blue Ridge and enter the Seminary. There was just time to pay one more call on the Drapers and other parishioners. So, one nice, warm day late in August, I saddled up the old white horse, which thoughtfully had been provided for my use by the School authorities, and rode up to the top of the small line of hills that marked the southern boundary of the hollow where the Drapers and other church members lived. There I reined the horse to a stop to give it a rest after the climb and to give me a chance to look around carefully over the area. The surrounding mountains shimmered in that haze so characteristic of the Blue Ridge Mountains. Down below, I was able to see the little farms and the log buildings about which the life of each family revolved. Around each clearing were large patches of thick woods where the people gathered their fire wood, hunted and engaged in other activities more or less legal. There was little breeze, and the leaves on the trees scarcely stirred. The only sounds were the barking of a couple of hounds and the occasional whirr of the jar flies. Everything looked quiet and peaceful.

I repeat that I looked around carefully. What I was looking for was smoke rising above the trees bordering a lovely little stream that twisted through the hollow. Such smoke was usually indicative of an industry upon which the government did not look with favor. Where there was smoke, there was a place to be stricken from my calling list, lest I cause acute embarrassment to myself and to certain worthies who were concerned for the moment with thirst for something beside spiritual refreshment. Seeing no smoke anywhere, I started the ride down into the little valley.

Pat Draper's place was the first I would come to after turning off on a short side road. A little distance behind the house was a wooded area through which the stream ran. The side road ended at Pat's wagon gate, which was kept latched to prevent the cows from wandering away. Anyone approaching from the main road was clearly visible and was usually spotted, for someone seemed to have the job of keeping a lookout to see "if company's coming".

Almost always when I arrived at the gate, I had been seen and one of the children would run down and open it for me. But this time it was different. I found Mrs. Draper there with her hands on the latch. She made no move to open the gate which was surprising. I doffed my hat and offered greetings to which she made no response. Normally she was a very voluble person. It seemed to me that my appearance was not the best thing that had happened to her that morning.

I said, "I thought that I would drop by today and see how Mr. Pat and you all are getting along. You know, I will be leaving these parts in a few days, and I wanted to pay another visit before I left."

That broke the spell and she replied, "Pat seen you coming and he sent me down to tell you he's real proud you thought to come to see him. But truth is, Pat ain't doing so good right now and, much as he wants you to visit a spell with him, he jest ain't up to it. So, he asked me to come and beg you to excuse him. He wants you to come again real soon when he feels better. Since you are thinking about going away soon, can you come next Tuesday? Come and eat a mess with us. Come and stay all day. We'll be right proud to have you."

I thanked her for her invitation, which I could not accept, and sent my best wishes to her husband. Taking my leave, I set out once more to make my calls. The next on my list was Hovey Powell. His first name was really Jehovah, but he didn't much look the part. He lived alone in a ramshackle cabin on a spur of High Top Mountain. He had not farmed his few acres for a long time, and by now briars and underbrush had quite taken over the place. The road up to his home was more like a gully, having been neglected with everything else, and my horse stumbled a time or two before we made the steep grade.

I found Hovey enjoying poor health as usual, though he looked quite well for all his seventy years. He was a hypochondriac with a lively imagination, which is a bad combination. He had every ailment he ever heard of and was never happier than when trying out some new cure for some ailment. On a prior visit, he was sure that he was just about done for and that he had no hope. Later it was reported that he had his top hair tied up in a knot "jest to keep my palate from falling".

He welcomed me fairly graciously and found me a suitable split-bottom chair. Then he sat down at a table on which there was an open faced watch beside a box of pills. Inquiring after his health, I was told that he had a "misery" and that the doctor had given him these little red pills and told him to take one every two hours without fail. Hovey was so glum that I had a difficult time carrying on a conversation with him. In bored desperation, I thought that I would try a neighborhood topic or two.

"I was sorry to find out that Pat Draper is ailing badly today," I ventured.

"Who told you that?" Hovey asked, raising his eyebrows in surprise.

"Why, Mrs. Pat did," I replied. "She met me at the gate and told me that Pat was too sick to have any company today. She asked me to come back next week."

At this, Hovey began to laugh so hard that I became quite puzzled how one man's woe could cause another sick man so much hilarity. Presently, he quieted down, wiped his eyes and said, still chuckling:

"I don't mean no harm but if you're going to be around these folks much, you got to git on to 'em. You can't believe everything they tell you. Now, look here, Pat ain't no sicker than usual. The trouble is that Pat and his boys is making a run today. And when a man is making likker, he sure don't want no preachers around."

Chapter 10

BUSHWHACKED!

One August afternoon in 1963, the Rev. K. Douglas Pitt and I stood vested in the center aisle of Cecil Memorial Mission to perform a ceremony that should have been done long before—that of deconsecrating the building. Thick layers of dust covered all the furniture. Cobweb streamers hung from the rafters. The altar had been stripped of its furnishings, and these were in use elsewhere. The rear wall was badly stained by a leak of long standing. The old organ once feebly supported the singing, but now it was voiceless. Mice and mold had completed its ruin. The bell had been removed from the tower, where years ago it used to summon the now vanished worshippers. This day, it lay rusting beside the front entrance. Somehow, it seemed that we were about to bury a corpse, which had lain here dead for decades while all concerned steadfastly refused to admit that its life had ebbed away.

I was acting under the authority of the Bishop of the Diocese, but I also had a very personal interest in the matter, because I could carry out unhindered what I had vainly attempted to do thirty years past. Candor demands the admission that the occasion provided me a degree of satisfaction quite inappropriate to the solemn event but which stemmed quite naturally from prior experience. It illustrated in a small way why church business is unlike any other business on the face of the earth.

Cecil Memorial Chapel, recently transformed into a residence, was located on U.S. Route 33, the Spotswood Trail, about three miles west of Stanardsville, the seat of Greene County, Virginia. It is a charming building with walls of native stone laid by an expert rock mason (Jason

Knight) who grew up in the Blue Ridge Mountain area. Even now it still retains most of its original loveliness.

The structure was a simple one with modest stained glass windows featuring color rather than tawdry design. On the left side of the chapel at the rear, a substantial square tower had been added when the building was constructed. The top served as a belfry and the lower portion as a small meeting room or a vesting room when needed by the clergy who ministered to the congregation. The nave was rectangular in shape and could accommodate about one hundred people at the most. The furniture was plain but serviceable. The bare floor was concrete, which made it easy to keep clean but also made it unbearably cold for the feet and knees of worshippers in winter. The entrance was slightly protected by a small portico. It was decorative, but it served little useful purpose.

Matters were quite different when the mission was established in 1910 by a vigorous pioneer priest, who had already opened several other stations in the Blue Ridge Mountains. In those days, the needs of the mountain people were especially great, not only in Greene County but throughout the whole region. Stark isolation was everywhere. Hill country was separated from low country, ridge from ridge, cove from cove, and hollow from hollow. Roads were very bad and virtually impassable in the winter. Public Schools were all but non-existent. Medical services were sketchy at best, and the few local doctors were overworked. Churches were few and far apart.

To help meet the desperate problems of a people living under extremely primitive conditions and condemned to ignorance and poverty, the Episcopal Church, over half a century ago, established a series of centers among the people to serve them where they lived. The typical center, or mission, consisted of a chapel, a school, a worker's house and a clothing bureau. Clergymen were placed in charge of groups of missions, and each mission had its resident lay worker and/ or school teacher.

Little is now remembered of these heroic workers, especially the women, who carried out their duties under trying conditions. Like the clergy, they not only directed Sunday Schools but conducted services and even buried the dead when the ministers were not available, which was often. Some taught day schools and others held classes in nutrition, cooking and home-making. Instruction in matters of sanitation and hygiene was routine. The sick and injured were visited and nursed. Not infrequently they were called on to arbitrate disputes, quell disturbances, and to deal with drunks. Above all, through teaching the Christian faith and ethic, they made great headway in persuading a proud independent, but lawless folk to have respect for the rights and safety of one another. In many areas, the number of killings and acts of violence declined impressively. Hundreds of children learned to read and write in the modest mission schools. It is worth mentioning that during the 1930s there were more Episcopalians in Greene County in proportion to the population than in any other county in the United States.

In return, these workers received little reward for grueling sacrifices except the gratitude of the mountain people and the satisfaction of knowing that life had been made more bearable and fuller for folk who, up to then, had been neglected, if not forgotten, by the society that claimed them as citizens. The lay salary range was between $30 and $50 a month. The clergy salary range was between $600 and $1,200 a year. But for the availability of clothing bureaus, and the gifts of family and friends, these dedicated ones would have lived in as dire poverty as the people they served.

With a need so great and a people so expectant of help, Cecil Memorial Mission, as well as several others, came into being as more and more members of the Episcopal Church became aware of the plight of the mountain people and supported the efforts of those who worked so hard to make life more decent and tolerable for them. A local farmer donated an acre of ground, and the Rev. Dr. Willis Cleaveland, the minister serving the area, making the most of slender resources, built a modest frame structure to serve as a chapel and schoolhouse. Afterward, an attractive log cabin was constructed as a residence for workers, and a deaconess was called to begin work in this new venture. Critics argued that the new mission was too close to Stanardsville and, since there was a church already in the county seat, the mission was not really needed.

In 1910, however, the three mile distance separating the two places might just as well have been thirty miles instead of three miles. The main road was not much better than a wagon road, and during the winter it was almost impassable at times. Sending children to school at the county seat was out of the question and so was attending church there, as most of the children and adults would have to walk coming and going. Then, too, there was a cultural gap between the people in the village and those living on the slopes of the Blue Ridge, who felt that they were looked down upon by the low-landers. The mountain folk were not hesitant in saying, "We don't hold with those folks down thar!" Soon it became clear that in the mountains then the people were served best in the communities where they felt at home.

As time went on, this mission, named for the little son of Dr. Cleaveland who died at the age of seven, prospered and all seemed well. The deaconess was followed ten years later by a very quiet woman worker who had an iron will, as many a cleric and business man discovered to his astonishment. The little school had as many pupils as it could handle, and the church services were well attended, considering the sparse population scattered over and in between the rising slopes of the blue hills. As the ministry of the mission touched more and more people, the frame school-chapel became quite inadequate for the demands made upon it. Obviously a new building was an imperative need, so dedicated people went to work.

For two years, the local people as they found time hauled tons of native stone by wagon and sleds to the site and pledged labor in lieu of money when the time came to start construction, since few dollars passed through their hands in the course of a year. Interested people in Richmond raised most of the cash required to see the project through. Thus, the stone chapel was completed and the first service was held in it on December 1, 1925.

A few years later, the rough, dirt, rock studded Spotswood Trail was widened and paved, attracting a growing flow of east-west traffic, and tourists began to discover some of the attractions of the region. The little stone church appealed especially to passers-by, many of whom stopped for a visit. Its setting, at its best in the springtime, was unexcelled. Coming up toward the west, the lush, open green pastures merged gradually with woodland as the land rose toward the crest of the Blue Ridge. One cannot forget the marvel of the clouds of white blossoms of thousands of dogwood trees spreading in every direction, dotted here and there by splotches of color where random pink dogwood trees added to the glory. It was and still is a scene challenged only in the autumn, when the brilliant colors of the changing leaves drew thousands every weekend to view their splendor.

Located as it was, "the sweet little church beside the Spotswood Trail" was fixed fondly in the memory of many, who would and did view with horror any suggestion of closing the mission. This was particularly true of the Episcopal Church women who had contributed generously to its building and support. Many pilgrimages were made to this spot on weekends and holidays in good weather, and glowing reports were brought back of the need and worth of this work, serving as it did a disadvantaged people.

On such brief visits, one would be little aware of the slow changes eroding the value of the enterprise. The development of good roads, the increasing use of automobiles, the establishment of the Shenandoah National Park, encouraged hundreds of families to begin leaving the hills in search of work and better standards of living. No longer was it necessary, as formerly, to situate churches and schools within walking distance of the people to be served. With a population declining and becoming more mobile, attendance on church services began to fall off gradually at first, then seriously. Also, the county school board, with the coming of paved roads, began to bus more and more children from outlying areas to centrally located schools. Thus, children were provided with schooling which the church had provided heretofore.

These factors were beginning to make themselves felt by the time I took charge of six mission stations in 1930, of which Cecil Memorial was one. It soon became evident that there was no need for the Episcopal Church to go to the expense of running a school at Cecil when the county school board was perfectly willing to transport the children the three miles into Stanardsville for their education. Those were the Depression years, and every dollar had to go where it was most needed. So with the consent of the Archdeacon and of the Board of Mountain Work, the school at Cecil Memorial was closed and the county took over.

There was much grumbling among the local people, who had become used to having their school close by and did not like change, quite overlooking the fact that they did not contribute a dime to the financial support of the school. The displeasure of the mission worker was intense, as she felt that the value and the importance of the mission were needlessly diminished. Such reactions were to be expected, but it was something of a surprise to get critical letters from many places in the Diocese, most of which showed ignorance of the situation.

As time went on, decline became acute, and I frequently discussed the situation with the Bishop of the Diocese, the Archdeacon, and the mission worker. My opinion was that the mission school should be closed, the missionary transferred to another post, and the property sold. The Bishop was noncommittal, the Archdeacon was reluctant, and the worker hostile. The affairs of the mission were not just of local concern. All over the Diocese, many had made contributions to this work and supported it also with a strong interest mixed with sentimentality. These would strenuously oppose such a step, I was informed.

So there the matter hung fire. Every other Sunday at three o clock I drove to Cecil Memorial for service, month in and month out. It became more and more of a depressing experience presiding over each increasingly dismal service as the congregation slowly faded away. One afternoon stands out vividly in memory. The congregation that day was a scanty band. Present were the worker, Demosthenes Deane, Ben Deane, two little girls and Ping Southard, who took care of the buildings. If there is ever a rock bottom, this was surely it.

In a mood of desperation, I reopened the whole question with my superiors. This time, I carefully prepared an imposing array of facts and statistics which seemed to say only one thing—the mission had served a wonderful purpose but now should be closed. The upshot was that both the Bishop and the Archdeacon conceded that there appeared to be no alternative. However, they ruled that in order to be fair, no final decision should be made until the people of the mission area were consulted and had a chance to express their opinions. This was only just, but did not seem important, since only a handful were left. They could now easily attend services in Stanardsville and, thus, relieve the Diocese of considerable expense and wasted manpower. After much discussion, it was agreed that on a Sunday afternoon, one month later, the Bishop, the Archdeacon, and I would meet with the congregation to discuss the future of the mission.

Following instructions, I first notified the worker, who accepted the news quietly. Then, I wrote to the very few people I counted as members of the chapel. All concerned took the notice calmly and, as far as I could see, the coming meeting was only a formality, so I dismissed it from my mind for the time being.

When the appointed day arrived, the Archdeacon drove out from Charlottesville to our rectory, bringing the Bishop with him for the midday meal. It was a pleasant occasion. The food was excellent, since my wife Constance was a superb cook, and the company mood was most congenial. All in all, the day promised to be a most satisfactory one.

In due time, we got into my car and started the three mile trip to Cecil Memorial encountering only light traffic on the highway. For one coming from the east, the mission is not in view of the motorist until he is nearly there after rounding a blind curve. Approaching this point, we were surprised to get into a traffic jam, such as was seldom, if ever, seen on this road. All around the bend, cars were parked on both sides, almost bumper to bumper. Slowing down, the only explanation that occurred to us at the moment was that there must be a bad accident up ahead, for this stretch of the road was rather dangerous.

However, as we got around the curve, we saw no sign of traffic difficulty but only some groups of people going into the chapel. We could not even get close to the entrance but had to drive above the lot and park in the lane running behind the old school building. The Bishop and the Archdeacon were surprised at the activity. As for myself, I could not believe what I saw.

We three walked to the chapel and entered. The building was packed. A glance at my superiors gave me a sinking feeling. Both had stopped still and were looking around with expressions of pleased astonishment. Also disheartening were the enquiring looks they shot at me sidelong. Right then I knew that I had lost. We made our way to the chancel and took our places. Calling the crowd to order, I introduced the Bishop and turned the meeting over to him, as agreed beforehand.

He chose a hymn to begin with and the singing rattled the rafters for the first time in years. During the hymn, I studied the congregation. Most were strangers to me. After the prayers, the Bishop stated the purpose of the gathering. Then he commented on the unusual attendance and asked if all present were members of this church. The register was produced, and several random samples indicated that most could claim membership at one time or another, even though right then few could claim membership on canonical grounds.

It was useless to bring this up. The attitude of the mountaineer churchman toward canon law was on a par with his attitude toward Federal law. It was an alien law imposed without the consent of the governed. As one of the hill people told me, "Church laws don't hold for us folks up here. They're made for those rich folks down thar in Richmond what don't know nothing about what suits us up here." So I decided to keep quiet after pointing out that, register or no register, a pathetically small percentage of those present ever showed up for services.

The Bishop then asked for an expression of opinion from anyone who wanted to speak. One after another passionately declared love for the mission and described what a tragedy it would be for Cecil Memorial to be closed. Some went so far as to say that if such a step were taken, "The Church would be doing the people dirt!" And so it went on until the Bishop ended the discussion and asked for a show of hands on the proposition, "Shall Cecil Memorial Mission be kept open?" It was no contest. Every hand went up but mine.

It was the mission worker's moment of triumph. Later, I found out what had happened. Without my knowledge, she had written to every person living, whose name was in the register and who had not transferred to another church. The latter was a technicality seldom observed in mountain ecclesiastical procedures. They were informed of the terrible thing being planned and were asked to get to the meeting, if humanly possible, in order to help save the dear chapel they all loved so much. So hither they came from Madison, Charlottesville, Elkton, Shenandoah, Luray, Ruckersville, Zion's Crossroads and Quinque.

In a kindly effort to let me down gently, the Bishop took those present to task for their neglect of religious duties, which had so discouraged their minister (who incidentally did not even know two-thirds of those present) and assured them that, in view of their loyalty and concern, Cecil Memorial Mission would not be closed. Then he called on those who wanted to show the minister that he could count on then in the future to stand up. All stood up. Then the Bishop dismissed the congregation with a blessing.

There is little to add. Two Sundays later, at the regular afternoon appointed time for service, I was once again at Cecil Memorial Mission. Of all those who had pledged their loyal support, who were present? There were the woman worker, Demosthenes Deane, Ben Deane, two little girls and Ping Southard.

Chapter 11

PAPER'S COME

Between the slopes of High Top Mountain and the Nortonsville Road, there were and still are many fertile farms where thrifty, hard-working owners had taken excellent care of their land. "The good earth" was not an empty term to them. It was their life, not to be wasted, nor allowed to bleed away into the Rapidan and South Anna Rivers like the blood of a father slain by the children he had nourished. They knew their land and loved it as the red, productive fields proclaimed. In tragic contrast were other farms that were slowly starving and died a little with every rain. Where crops flourished, the owners were usually Dunkards, a group of German-American Baptists. They were vigorous, frugal, deeply religious people, self-reliant and asking favors from no one. Few could be called well-to-do, but none knew want. Each walked head high, paid debts promptly, and held closely to one particular rule of life, "Do as you would be done by."

They were courteous and hospitable. Visitors were welcomed warmly. If a visit extended into mealtime, an extra place was set at the table as a matter of course, and a declination would be taken amiss. The dishes served, a dietician's despair, were virtually those found on every table in the area. Meats and potatoes were fried swimming in grease. Vegetables were usually over-cooked with a little seasoning added. Greens were boiled generally with a piece of smoked hog-jowl or middling for flavor. For a beverage there was always fresh milk and also coffee boiled in a pot into which egg shells were dropped before serving to settle the grounds.

Biscuits or cornbread filled out the meal. Dessert commonly was pie and a piece of pickle.

Few of these people were conversationalists. Work was too pressing and time was too short for small talk. As a result, they were often mistakenly thought to be secretive, cold, and unfriendly. Though reserved, they were neighborly after their fashion, and one could find them mingling freely with crowds at church, auctions, cattle shows, and on court days. Whenever there was sickness, misfortune or want in the area, none responded more quickly nor more generously than the Dunkards.

Denominational lines in the county were sharply drawn in the matter of doctrine, and social customs were considered dictated by divine law. However, as I visited throughout the western part of Greene County, I discovered that I was welcome in almost any home regardless of religious affiliation. In fact, when I called on my members in a particular section or community, I was expected to drop in at the others as a neighborly gesture. Thus, I gained many friends, whom I came to admire greatly, outside of what would have been a rather small circle, and at whose hands I received many kindnesses.

One of these was a Dunkard patriarch. His principles were as rigid as his backbone. He stood straight and tall for all his seventy years. His full head of hair was iron grey, and, as the custom of his sect two generations ago, he wore a full beard but his upper lip was shaven. His clothes were somber and were fastened with tapes instead of buttons. He very seldom smiled. He wore a black hat with a wide brim but with a low crown. His muscles were hard and his hands as tough as leather from decades of hard labor. He prided himself that he could still keep up with any man with a hoe or behind the plough.

His farm had the appearance of a tribal community with three generations settled on it. Three married sons and one married daughter built separate houses on the home place, and the five families worked the large farm together. There seemed to be a child behind every bush, and the whole area appeared to be a busy, happy spot, definitely under the benign sway of the grandfather, who held the group to the customs of his church as they were followed half a century ago. This arrangement existed only because of the force of the patriarch's personality, and most of the members of the family scattered a few years after his death because the little community was not economically viable with its limited resources and growing numbers.

The younger men of the family did not have beards but dressed as did the elder. The women wore simple, full length dresses with fastenings of tapes instead of buttons and pins. The use of jewelry, perfumes, cosmetics and any kind of personal adornment was forbidden. They combed their hair straight back and gathered it up at the nape of the neck in a knot or bun. Women and girls then had no hats but all wore the old fashioned poke bonnet. Alcoholic beverages, dancing, card playing, and frivolous amusement were under the ban. To hear their preachers, it would seem that anything that gave pleasure was a sin and displeased God. They belonged to a tough and honorable breed of people, but few smiled and for them, life had a melancholy hue. This spartan life has changed markedly now, and even then, the young were beginning to rebel and to long for a life with more grace and less law.

However, it was a privilege to know this family group, and I never failed to pay a visit when I was in the vicinity. All who could be spared from their duties would come into the house and "visit a spell" with the preacher. Since we did not have the same church ties, the conversation dealt mainly with the weather, crops, places, and people. I had the feeling that I was to them a peripatetic newspaper, as I travelled over a fairly wide territory. They were anxious to hear what was going on in other parts of the county, and no item of news or gossip was too trivial for discussion.

In the 1920s, in many places, few of the older people had any education to speak of. A great number of those who could read and write did so with considerable difficulty. Their children, on the other hand, were beginning to benefit from an improved school system and to enjoy advantages denied their parents. Elders often depended upon their boys and girls, who had a few years of schooling, to read to them and to handle their correspondence. The girls, incidentally, were far better at this than the boys. What happened during one of my visits to my Dunkard friends illustrates this situation well.

It was afternoon on a pleasant summer day when I stopped by. Word went out "Preacher's here", and the few who could leave their chores came in for a chat. Most of them sat on the floor of the sparsely furnished living room. There were no rugs or carpets and never had been. On the walls were a couple of faded color prints of farm scenes and the usual gaily colored calendar from some feed or lumber company. There were two rocking chairs and three straight back chairs. The sheet-iron stove, which could come up quickly to red-hot in cold weather, had not been removed for the summer. Above it was the mantelpiece, whose underside had been a bit scorched when the stove once heated up too quickly. It was decorated by a few trinkets and the inevitable Kewpie doll probably obtained at some county fair. In the center was a clock with a golden oak casing about fifteen inches high. The clock was not running and would not again soon since there were no facilities for repairing timepieces nearer than Charlottesville.

After we had chatted for twenty minutes or more, the twelve year old granddaughter looked out of the window and said, "Here comes the mailman." She excused herself, went out and returned with the <u>Greene County Record</u>, a modest, four page paper, which was eagerly looked forward to every Wednesday. Then the grandfather explained to me that it was the family custom for everyone to come in, no matter what they were doing, and all listen to the news together. He hoped that I would stay and listen also, especially since maybe I could add something to what the paper said because I got around so much and knew so many people.

Few had any use for any other paper. There were those who did subscribe to the Charlottesville <u>Daily Progress</u>, the <u>Washington Post</u>, and the <u>Richmond Times Dispatch</u>. These were luxuries and supposedly only rich people could afford them but this was their business. Excuses could be made for such strange tastes since such publications did carry news of surrounding counties and of the politics of the state. Also, they brought news of the baseball world and particularly of the Washington Senators, a team that was mildly popular in the county. Cast-off Sunday editions were in demand because of the advertisements as well as reading matter. But there was another attraction—they were good for wallpaper and in many a mountain home the chief room was decorated with rotogravure sections and the comic sheets. For a while, I subscribed to <u>The New York Times</u>. This was never understood, and I was told often that there wasn't any use in "knowing about folks nobody around here ever heard about". In general, the word "newspaper" meant the <u>Greene County Record</u>.

With its arrival, the call went out, "Paper's come!" The older children and the men who had been busy in the field came into the house, pausing on the way to wash their faces and hands and to get a drink of cool water. After they straggled into the living room, some stood and the rest sat on the floor in a semi-circle. Then the twelve year old granddaughter placed a chair facing the group, sat down and began to read. These little newspapers are too often ridiculed by sophisticates, who have little understanding of the void that such homey and chatty publications fill in the lives of most of their subscribers, whose range of interest did not go much beyond the borders of their counties or settlements. Within circumscribed areas, little things look large, and seeming trivialities have great importance. Readers learn of births and deaths. They learn of auctions, livestock sales, coming fairs and farm shows. Above all, they are interested in people, and any news about people is big news.

That afternoon, each bit of news was listened to intently as the young girl read deliberately and carefully. The grandfather was somewhat deaf and kept a hand cupped to his "good ear". Now and then, when his granddaughter wearied a little and dropped her voice, the old man would say, "Now, child, catch your breath and read that piece again. I don't aim to miss nothing." Occasionally, during the two hour family ritual, she would get spells of rest when some items aroused special comment and attention.

As far as memory serves, news and remarks ran something like this:

> "Mr. Sterling Shifflett was bitten by a snake two weeks ago while cutting fodder and has been very sick. We hear that he is up and around now and hope that he will be in good health soon."

"Wonder what kind of snake it was."

"Obliged to have been a moccasin or a rattle snake. 'Tain't no other kinds 'round these parts what kin poison."

"Spose I git snake bit. What do I do for it?"

"Lots of folks say you look for somebody what's got a hart stone, and put it on the bite to dreen out the pizen."

"Who knows whar to find a man like that real quick? Aunt Lartie says to cut the place deep and soak the wound with coal oil."

"Most people say you cure snake bite by drinking a pint of likker."

"Don't talk like that, boy. Listen to your grandpa. Don't even name likker 'round this house. Likker's a sin and never cures nothing. Keep areading, Mary."

> "Mr. Henry Morris from near Dyke stopped by the office when he came in to the courthouse the other day. He brought us some Irish potatoes he had just dug and they were nice as any we had seen this year. Mr. Morris said that they would have been better if the weather had not been so dry. We are always glad to have friends come in to see us and many times they have some news which we can use for the paper."

"If that ain't jest like Henry. I bet his wife planted 'em, raised 'em, and dug 'em, and Henry takes all the credit. What can you expect of a man from Bacon Hollow anyway?"

"Tom, you know better than to talk against somebody like that. You ain't sure what you said is so. It jest ain't right to bear false witness. You know what the Good Book says about that. Then, too, those folks in Bacon Hollow are as fine people as you'll find any place."

"I didn't mean no harm, ma! I was jest talking. But I got a notion that if you poke around some, you'll find I ain't too wrong. We better git back to the paper reading. We'll be here the rest of the day at this rate. What's the next thing, Mary?"

> "We hear that there was a good rain down around Quinque last Friday and we are glad for the people down there. We are having a drought this month and the churches are praying for rain. Some people from High Top told us that men are cutting branches from locust trees to feed livestock because pastures are so short. That is a bad sign, but maybe we shall get a better season yet."

"Well, it looks like them that pray ain't no better off than them what don't. How come?"

"When it comes to weather, son, everybody got to take the same chances. The church elder's field gits as wet or dry as the backslider's. How about it, sister Ruth? You lead at prayer meetings a lot. Maybe you can explain it to Tom."

"All I know is, what will be, will be, Tom. It looks to me like somebody must be powerful at prayer around Quinque. Pa, I been aiming to ask you for a long time, why did they give that funny name to Quinque?"

"I don't rightly know, daughter. I done heard that it's some kind of foreign word. Anyway, before my time, it used to be the fifth stop of the stage coaches out of Charlottesville towards the Valley. They changed horses thar and them what was hungry could git a bite to eat. At least, that's what the old folks told me. All right, Mary."

> "The Temple Hill Methodist Church will begin its
> revival next Sunday with two services, the first at eleven
> and the second at three o'clock. The ladies of the church
> will serve a benefit lunch on the grounds at one o'clock
> if the weather permits. Everyone is invited."

"Grandpa, let's surprise 'em real good by us all showing up next Sunday. They won't know how to take it, 'specially if you let go with some of your loud 'Amens' during preaching."

"Buster, don t you go poking fun at church doings. Religion ain't nothing to laugh at. It's mighty serious, and you'd be a lot better off if you tried to understand it instead of fidgeting and sniggering with the other boys in the back of the church. If you'd learn to listen, you might hear something worthwhile to make a man of you."

"I guess you are right, grandpa. They tells me that those Methodists give you purty good fried chicken and don't charge too much neither. That ought to make it worthwhile going."

"Stop right there, Buster. You're talking jest to hear yourself talk and I kin git plain tired of it. We all are going to our church Sunday whar we belong, and we are all going to eat at home afterwards whar we belong. Let the Methodists alone. They never done you no harm."

It was easy to see that the family thoroughly enjoyed this weekly newspaper ritual, and it was one of the bonds strongly uniting the group. Differences of opinion from time to time led to bickering that was more feigned than real and served more to relax the tension of listening than to create dissension. Twelve year old Mary was the star of the occasion, and she enjoyed her importance to the fullest. Without her, there would be no sessions until some of the younger children learned to read as well as she could and that would not be soon. This is now a thing of the past, but there was a period during which it could well be said of the adults of yesterday, "And a little child shall lead them"

Chapter 12

HERE COMES THE BRIDE

In most of the rural counties of Virginia, the best time to see friends and acquaintances is on court day. Then almost everyone, who is physically able and can get off from work, heads for the county seat. Some have business with or are summoned to court. Some come to patronize the limited shopping facilities, or to lay in supplies purchased at feed and grocery stores. Some bring in horses for trading and occasionally other livestock to sell. Crowds are attracted by auctions advertised in advance and by itinerant entertainers of dubious skill but always welcome. Ever present is the medicine man with his side-show spiel, shills, extracting from spellbound rustics hard earned cash for herb medicines, liberally laced with alcohol, and far inferior to those that the country people could cook up for themselves if they had a mind to. There was always a chance for excitement such as a fight or when a deputy chases a thimble-rigger or a pick pocket. At times, somewhere around the fringes of crowds, one could find furtive operations: cock fights, crap games, stolen goods for sale, and offerings of illegal whiskey. To people with little color in their lives, court day came as an exciting break in their grim monotony.

Court day in Greene County differed from the general pattern only because of its size. Since it is such a small county, one could find any person he was looking for within two hundred yards of the courthouse square. For a minister, who found shaking hands with the members of a multiple church circuit a useful practice, court day was a godsend, and it nearly always took a great strain off his pastoral conscience. I found it very useful during the early 1930s when I had charge of six mountain missions scattered over a wide area that made house calls most difficult, especially when the mountaineers never considered a "pop" call a visit. A visit was for all day, or at least long enough "to eat a mess". They were a most hospitable folk whose homes were open to a caller. Under these conditions, a pastor found it impossible to report to his superiors a respectable number of calls during a given year.

One spring court day, I was mingling with the usual throng and having a wonderful time greeting people right and left, when I felt a tug at my coat sleeve. Turning, I saw a small group of people at my side. In front was a young man of about nineteen and a girl sixteen years of age, both of whom seemed quite embarrassed. Behind them stood the parents of each and in the background a few of their kin folk. I knew them well and, with a beaming smile, I shook hands all around but this only added to their embarrassment.

Presently, one of the fathers said, "These young'uns want to git married. Kin you do it?"

"Of course, I can," I replied. "Where's the license?"

"Here it is", said the mother of the bride-to-be, whipping an envelope out of a battered handbag.

Looking it over, everything seemed legally in order, and both sets of parents declared that they had given their consent to the marriage of these minors. Since my church was close by in the village, I led the party into the building and showed them where to sit while I lit the candles on the Holy Table and put on my vestments. This done, I positioned the boy and the girl in the customary places for a bride and a groom and then appointed a kinsman and kinswoman to be best man and maid of honor.

Proceeding with the service, I came to the exchange of the promises, and when I told the groom what to say I ran into trouble. He seemed to misunderstand me, he stammered, he mispronounced the words, and he seemed to be reluctant to take the bride's hand. In general his behavior appeared overly bashful. That mountain folk tended to be shy in formal situations, I knew well, but this was ridiculous. At last, we got through the service. I blessed the couple and sent them on their way. Then I looked down toward the front door of the church, and there stood the sheriff! All became clear—too clear! I had been trapped into officiating at a "shotgun wedding".

I did not appreciate the situation one bit. For such an occasion, a justice of the peace would have been sufficient to preside over a transaction that had no religious content. There was also another reason why it was my practice to refuse to officiate at such weddings. Under the canon law of the Episcopal Church, its clergy was forbidden to solemnize any marriage where there was coercion or duress. Both were certainly present in this case and, being young and unseasoned then, the business weighed a bit heavily on my conscience.

Not long afterward, my bishop, the Rt. Rev. H. St. George Tucker, D.D., came to make his regular visitation to my mission field and stayed overnight at the rectory in Stanardsville, as was his custom. After supper, he and I went into the living room, while my wife put the children to bed, and sat before the open wood fire. The bishop took out a cigar and lit it. When he had it going satisfactorily, he relaxed and asked if there were any problems I wanted to discuss with him. So I laid my worries about the sheriff sponsored wedding before him and sought his counsel. The bishop considered the matter pensively for a few puffs while looking at the fire. Shortly, he smiled and said, "Don't worry about it anymore. The boy certainly did not give his free consent to the marriage, but he did give his full consent to the act that made the marriage necessary. I wouldn't give the affair another thought, but in the future keep your eyes open. Up here, you are apt to run into these cases quite often."

And he was so right.

There was a time, generations ago, when mountain communities were quite isolated, that many men and women "took up with each other" without formality. It was not uncommon for a couple to start living together with the understanding that when it was convenient and they had the time and the money they would journey to the courthouse, buy a license, look up a preacher, and legalize their union. Others would decide to waive formalities until a minister came through the hills and have him "to marry us", often with their children present witnessing the ceremony. However, convenient seasons were slow in presenting themselves, and it might be years before a minister of the Gospel found his way into the far coves and hollows. Those who had been married properly would disapprove of these irregular relationships but also would tolerate them as a situation that could not be helped.

In a number of areas, it was difficult to discover which pairs were legally married and which were not, especially since most of them lived together in what appeared to be stable unions. There were even cases where one man would be taking care of two women in separate houses, built practically side by side, raising a family by each with no disharmony evident between his two mates.

This situation continued until in time the church and the law made their appearance as constant rather than fitful forces. Evangelists in growing numbers penetrated farther and farther into the deeper recesses of the mountains, fulminating against unbelief and the all too evident sins of the flesh. With whiffs of good news laced with brimstone, emotions were stirred to almost hysterical levels. Crowds were brought to their knees and then down into the baptismal waters. So deeply did such methods take hold on the minds and feelings of mountain folk that to this day many are still convinced that there is no conversion, no hope of eternal salvation, without seizures of emotional ecstasy followed up with baptism by immersion only.

Whatever may be said with regard to the validity of such types of religious appeal and experience, they did fill a drab emptiness in the lives of the people who had few emotional outlets beyond drink, sex, and outbursts of violence. Religious leaders thus gained a strong influence over the people and set about trying to straighten out their moral kinks, but it was hard going. They did reduce a measure of the violence, succeed in teaching some respect for the law, and make some inroads on the problem of drunkenness, thereby improving markedly the conditions of community life.

With equal zeal, the ministers tackled those who were "living in sin", persuading them to get married properly and offering to hold marriage services free of charge and even putting up the money for licenses when the men could not do so. In this effort they met with considerable success. But there were those who resisted this persuasion as an unwarranted intrusion into their personal affairs by folks who were too nosey for their own good. The bulk of these capitulated when told that their refusal would be reported to the courts and that law officers would be calling on them in due time. Even so, there were holdouts, and the marital status, if any, of many couples was vague.

As time passed, however, wedlock became the accepted norm and the informal unions the exception. Still the problems of fornication and adultery remained to the extent they do in most communities. In the minds of not a few, there was doubt as to their paternity. A case in point was that of a young man who was summoned to court as a witness by the prosecution in the matter of a knife fight. His father had preceded him to the witness stand. When the son had given his name, the commonwealth's attorney asked if the two were kin. The reply was, "Yes, we's kin. He's my pa—I reckon."

There were unfortunate pregnancies still among the older girls and young unmarried women, but the matter came not to be treated so lightly as in past years. Many babies could be dated from apple picking time, apple butter boilings, and camp meetings when large numbers of young and old gathered. Caught up in close association and times of frolicking and considerable excitement, not a few of the younger set would slip away into the darkness out of sight and away from the attention of their elders who were otherwise occupied. The term "apple butter baby" was occasionally only too descriptive.

In these cases, the man named by the girl, or woman, was expected "to do right by her". Sometimes he did, and sometimes he was pursued by the sheriff armed with a warrant sworn out by the woman's kinsmen. There were times when a person driving from one county to the next might see young men loafing at a country store or on a roadside close to the county line. If he was well acquainted, he would recognize one or two of them as persons who had gotten a girl or young woman "in trouble" and were staying as close to home and friends as possible but just out of reach of the law until the affair blew over. There were forced marriages all right but in the area where I worked, nuptials at the point of a gun existed largely in legend, or in poor jokes. I never knew of a bona fide case in all my experience, except one and that happened to a noted Methodist minister in Charlottesville on a quiet summer afternoon.

He was clearing his office desk in the parsonage, preparing to go to a baseball game. His secretary was typing the last of the letters and would be going home shortly. The phone rang. The secretary answered and handed her employer the phone (that was before the buzz-button era). He took it with a feeling that there would be no baseball for him today, and he was right. It was the local social service worker requesting his aid in handling a problem for some people from the Ragged Mountains, who were with her then,

It was a matter only too familiar to the pastor. A boy had "gotten a girl in trouble". Her mother had the boy jailed and taken to court. The judge decided that if the boy would agree to marry the girl, he would release him from jail. The condition was accepted, and a court order was issued. The social worker was with the couple and relatives right then and needed the help of the pastor, who reluctantly consented to meet with the parties and see what he could do. Such cases bothered him. He was not just a "marrying parson" and wanted to know more before agreeing to officiate, and so insisted that the social worker come immediately with the group to the parsonage,

Shortly thereafter, a "flivver" rattled noisily up the street and parked, followed by the social worker. A motley group soon assembled in the parlor, led by the social worker. The bride and groom-to-be seemed to be very young and naive and very embarrassed. There were two men dressed in clean shirts and overalls whom the minister guessed to be the fathers of the couple and a woman, who held the boy's hand, obviously his mother. Dominating the group was a grim purposeful woman wearing a gingham dress and a flowered poke-bonnet which nearly hid her face. She brought up the rear and was carrying a shotgun.

The clergyman stopped her at the door and admonished her,

"Sister, leave the gun in the car. We are all friends here."

"Mr. Preacher, somebody'll steal it," she replied. "When you git out among strangers, you never know when you'll need it, things being what they is. I don' t mean no harm."

"I'll tell you what to do. Leave the gun right here propped against the door jamb out of the way. That's right. Now here's a rocking chair where you can sit and keep an eye on it. Sit down and rest yourself while I talk to the lady you came with."

She did so with much grumbling and rocked vigorously back and forth—back and forth.

After seeing to it that the others were also seated, he took the social worker aside and asked for the details of the affair, which she supplied as far as she knew them,

First, the two families were not on good terms and were trying to solve the problem as best they knew how. The two youngsters had little education and were not very bright. The boy could not read or write. The girl could with difficulty. At that time Judge Lindsey of Chicago was making propaganda for "companionate marriage" with great enthusiasm, and the papers were full of it. The girl read the reports with great effort and shared the information with the boy. She became pregnant, and her mother went on the warpath and had the boy jailed, who now agreed to the marriage, and the judge would be obliged if the minister consented to perform the ceremony. The social worker urged the minister to do so, saying that she believed that the marriage had a fair chance for success and might make peace between the two families.

The pastor was persuaded and examined meticulously the court order and the license and instructed the bride and groom to stand before him. He also appointed his wife and secretary as witnesses. The bride's mother kept rocking nervously. All went well until the minister came to the part of the marriage ceremony where he said, as directed, "If any man can show just cause why these two cannot be lawfully married, let him stand up or forever hold his peace." At that the bride's mother sprang from the rocking chair, seized the gun, pointed it at the clergyman, snarling "Now you marry these two or I'll shoot you." A gasp went up from those present, who froze with alarm at the beldam's fury. But the pastor faced her squarely and said quietly, "Sister, you sit down and stop pointing that gun at me and I will proceed. Otherwise, I will not." She stared at him for a moment, lowered the gun and sat down. A relieved sigh went up and the service went on.

After this no more surprises seemed possible but there was a sequel months later in the form of a phone call from the social worker. A young man appeared at the home of the couple and claimed that he was the true father of the baby, and the shotgun bride had run away with him to parts unknown leaving the erstwhile groom feeling foolish.

Women of convenience strayed through the region now and then, and occasionally "ran a house" until forced to leave by public disapproval, or by the law, or most often by lack of profit. No one seemed to know where they came from or where they went. Only one stayed, according to common knowledge. She was called "Old Bess" and apparently she had been around for several years. Gossip had it that once she had been "a mighty good looking woman", but by my time what charms she might have boasted had long since vanished. Broken and haggard, she had no certain dwelling place and lived on the pity of the mountain people who gave her food and old clothing.

Old Bess wandered here and there over the hill sections of two or three counties, stopped by whim at homes where she would stay for a few days, and then wander on. No one refused her. When well meaning persons would remonstrate with a husband and wife who had given Old Bess harbor more than once, they got the same answer nearly every householder gave:

"I jest can't turn away somebody that comes to my door. I know she is dirty and awful but she's got nowhere to turn. I can't shut the door in her face. The Good Book teaches us to do as we would be done by. They say letting her in is bad for the children but they got to learn things some day. She don't stay long nohow. Anyways I can't tell her to go away and face my God."

Now and then, when holding services, I would see her sitting on a back pew, having slipped in after worship began. She was always attentive and joined in the hymns lustily. But just before the service ended, she would leave as quietly as she came and be nowhere in sight when the congregation disbanded. The few times I was able to have some conversation with her, she did not have much to say beyond answering questions and gave the impression of being dull witted. I did discover that she had a prodigious memory and startled me by her ability to quote passages at length from the Bible.

On one occasion, I was called to hold a burial service in a private graveyard not far from Kinderhook. A goodly crowd gathered for the funeral, including many of my church members. After vesting, I conferred with the bereaved family about their wishes for the service and they asked that we sing "Jesus, lover of my soul", as it was a favorite hymn of the deceased. This created a problem, since I had not been informed in advance that music would be wanted and had not brought a hymnal along. Worse, I did not know the hymn by heart. I called on three of my lustiest men singers present to help me "heist the tune". Neither did they remember all the hymn, I quickly discovered, but they thought that together we could get the words "all writ down" and then manage very well.

I did have a pencil and happily there were two blank pages in the back of my copy of The Book of Common Prayer which could be used. We had no trouble with the first verse and started briskly into the second:

> "Other refuge have I none,
> Hangs my helpless soul on thee;
> Leave, ah leave me not alone
> Still support and comfort me!"

At this point we stalled and could get no farther, no matter how much we hummed the tune and repeated the last line I had written down. At this juncture, a woman's voice beside me said, "What you're looking for is:

> "All my trust on thee is stayed;
> All my help from thee I bring."

I looked around and there was Old Bess, who, unnoticed, had joined our little group. She tapped my prayer book with a grubby forefinger and said:

"Did you git that writ? No? Well git it down. Now write

> "Cover my defenseless head
> With the shadow of thy wing."

"Here's the last verse:

> "Plenteous grace with thee is found,
> Grace to cleanse from every sin;
> Let the healing streams abound,
> Make and keep me pure within."

"I'm going too fast for you, ain't I? I'll wait for you to ketch up. Ready? I'll go slow so's you can ketch up:

> "Thou of life the fountain art,
> Freely let me take of thee;
> Spring thou up within my heart,
> Rise to all eternity."

With her aid, for she also helped to lead the singing, the burial service was conducted to the satisfaction of the family. At its close, Old Bess walked away and I never saw her again.

In that same general area, there lived a couple without benefit of clergy, who were the despair of their neighbors and also of church workers. They had been living together for several years and had five children, of whom the oldest was fifteen and the youngest two years old. Many efforts had been made to get them to do "the right thing", but to no avail. The woman was willing but her mate would always reply, "I want to study it some." When I came into the region, my church members brought the case to my attention and were quite insistent that I waste no time in persuading the man to give the woman and the children a name.

So I tried my luck and had several conversations with the pair. As before, the man was the problem. He did not consent. Neither did he refuse. He multiplied excuses. First it was, "I ain't finished my plowing yit." After that "well—maybe." Next, "Soon's I git my corn crop laid by we'll see." Then, "It jest don't suit right now." At this, I surrendered. There is nothing so final as a mountaineer's "It don't suit."

There the matter stood until a brisk young seminary student was sent out to help me during the following summer. It was not long before the problem was put up to him, especially since he roomed in the mission house not far from where the pair lived. Immediately, he drove in to Stanardsville to talk with me about the scandal. His conversation had an undertone of reproof that I had let the affair go on so long without settling it. I sketched in the background, but my version did not convince him at all. Anon, he asked me for permission to see what he could do, which was gladly granted.

A week later, he was back highly elated. All was settled. A date had been set for the wedding ten days later, provided that it did not conflict with my schedule. That was no problem. So off he dashed. A few days later, he returned. It seemed that the prospective groom had no money to buy a license, so if I could advance my assistant three dollars, he would go right over to the county clerk's office and get the license. I gave him the three dollars and he left saying that he would phone me when to come out for the wedding. A week went by and there was no phone call. So I drove out to the mission to see what was causing the delay. It appeared that the hesitant groom had no clothes "fittin' for a wedding", and he was too proud to stand up before the preacher dressed in his old "overhauls".

Those were the days of the Great Depression and, like millions of others, I did not have much of a wardrobe, but there was a black suit of which I had wearied, that should fit the gentleman's needs and to which he was more than welcome. This cheered the student immensely, so he followed me home in his car, got the suit, and returned to the hollow. That evening he phoned me that all was set and that he would call me when to come out. I congratulated him and I told him that I would he waiting for his summons,

Several days passed and there was no phone call. In spite of my intense curiosity it seemed best to let the seminarian handle whatever there was to be handled. In due time, a very crestfallen young divine came to the rectory. He reported that he had delivered the suit and that the grateful recipient declared that he was now ready to "do the right thing". The next day it was discovered that the groom-to-be had disappeared, leaving no word. Only yesterday had any news been received and that through a friend of his who had encountered him near the little valley town of Shenandoah, wearing the black suit. It seemed that he had taken the suit and that night had walked over the pass into the next county where he could "dodge" safely in case anybody took a notion to swear out a warrant. Anyway, he sent back this message, "Thar ain't going to be no marrying. The 'Piscopal Church ain't got no right to expect me to marry a woman like that."

Chapter 13

A CHICKEN IN EVERY POT

"A chicken in every pot,
A car in every garage."

Republican National Committee Slogan
1928 Presidential Campaign

By lowland standards, life for the Blue Ridge people used to be a continual depression, especially in the 1920s and 1930s. When I knew them then, they were insufficiently clothed, they were ill-fed and undernourished, their general health was poor, and the infant mortality rate was high. They had to work cruelly hard to eke out a meager living tilling their rocky farms, caring for their livestock, hunting and fishing, cutting wood, fighting forest fires, and doing odd jobs on low pay when jobs could be found. Want and semi-starvation were constant threats.

When the Great Depression clamped its ruthless grip on the nation in 1930, the mountain folk were better prepared to cope with it than most, because they had gone without so much for so long. Bad as the economic situation was, they were not too much worse off, until the dreadful droughts of 1930 and 1932, which devastated fields, pastures, and gardens and made life grim indeed.

Each day that passed mocked the Republican promise of "A chicken in every pot, and a car in every garage". At that time, among the mountain people, scarcely anyone owned a car, or even hoped to own one. Later, they would have been glad to settle for enough feed to keep healthy the horse or the mule they had in the stable, not to mention their cows and hogs. As for chickens, few were destined for any pot in the hills. They were a source for ready money, meager though it was. Eggs brought nine cents a dozen in cash, and ten cents a dozen in trade. Chickens were worth only nine cents a pound in cash and ten cents a pound in trade.

Those that reached the pot were scarcely luxury items. They were scrawny, sorry birds at best. During the green months, chickens were turned loose to scratch and fend for themselves around the yard, the fields, and nearby woods, with their fare supplemented by the few table scraps available. In the cold months, when egg production should have been high, hens were fed mostly scraps and grain since corn was cheap and wheat was fifty cents a bushel. Few families could afford to buy laying mash, and consequently egg and meat production was below any reasonable standard. In the need for cash, the best and heaviest hens were sold off leaving the worst for the table, so flocks declined in quality and numbers.

To build them up, good "settin' eggs" were in great demand but not in sufficient supply locally. Those who could afford the necessary cheap oil brooders could get day old chicks at the hatchery near the county seat. It was pathetic to see some people in the area hang around the hatchery when a brood was due to be taken from the incubators. They came to beg for the eggs that had not hatched out with the rest. These would be carried home in a warm container and examined in a heated place, usually the kitchen. Those that sounded as though the chicks were alive but not strong enough to peck through the shell were opened carefully, the weaklings gently extracted, placed in a covered box back of the kitchen stove and nursed like babies. Enough survived to make the time and trouble worthwhile but their quality was poor. The mountain chicken was at best a miserable emblem for a presidential campaign, and most of the people were willing to forget the promise of the Great Engineer, even though most of the qualified voters in the Blue Ridge cast their votes for him. They were happy enough to have some pork for their pots, or even a little red meat, if any could be found.

Finding something, however, became a real problem when the searing drought of 1930 was added to the worsening Depression. After a dry spring, there was little rain in Greene County from early June until October. The weather was particularly hot during the whole time. Steadily the green of summer turned to a desert-like brown. Springs and wells began to go dry, and streams flowed sluggishly as they became shallow; and the rocks, bared by lowering water levels, bleached like bones in a dying land. Pastures failed as the grass burned under a searing sun. More and more could be heard the agonized bellowing of cattle for food and water at a time when pasturage normally should have been belly high and water abundant. One sign of a losing battle was seeing mountain men hacking down locust saplings and branches from locust trees, and dragging them home to feed horses and cows. This could not go on, and many a man sold off his livestock because he could not buy enough feed to keep his animals.

Fortunately, the spring crops had matured before the drought became dangerous. The main cash crop of cabbage yielded well and was sold on a good market, but after that, all the news was bad. Stunted corn withered in the fields, and even in the low grounds scarcely a nubbin could be found. One by one the gardens perished and people had to fall back on supplies of canned goods left over from the winter. In the woods, the death rate among birds and small animals was heavy. Underbrush turned yellow, berry bushes made no yield, and scores of glorious oaks perished. Underfoot, the ground cover was dry like excelsior. A spark, a lighted cigarette carelessly discarded, could set off a fire like an explosion, and there was little with which to fight it.

Each morning, we all looked toward the mountains across the drab fields hoping for signs that the pitiless weather might break. But morning after morning, the burning sun rose in a clear sky and scorched its way over a devastated earth until it was swallowed up in a night nearly as hot and punishing as the day. We looked for a cloud in the sky, but the only cloud we saw was a cloud of smoke over the mountains where fires never seemed to die out. Week after week the pillar of smoke hovered over the hills, our spirits flagged, and the cheerfulness with which we tried to greet our neighbors became more and more forced.

As fast as one fire was put out, another broke out in the powder dry woods. The fire wardens got little rest but had no trouble at all in hiring sufficient men to fight and to contain the blazes. Ugly rumors floated around the county. Out of them jelled one suspicion that would not die down: the fires were set by men desperate for work and for money, knowing that as long as the weather stayed dry, they would be employed. However, nothing could be proved. It was also known that, in spite of all that game wardens could do, game was heavily hunted out of season, and almost all the fish were taken from the mountain streams by dynamiting. Public morale sank lower and lower as the weary days dragged by. A peculiar indifference to bad news seemed to set in because hardly anything else was expected. Continuous prayers were offered for rain in the churches, and the "Amens" were never more emphatic or sincere.

The next year brought relief with abundant rain and excellent growing conditions, but there was no improvement in the economy in the mountain area. Food was abundant but money was scarce and the market for produce was listless. At times, farmers who hauled their vegetables, poultry, and eggs to towns and cities could not dispose of them at any price. There were seasonal jobs on farms in our area, but at inhuman wages paid by those who battened on the misery of the poor. Many a man worked ten hours a day for fifty cents and furnished his own lunch just to get some ready money.

Bad as matters were, the Greene County people seemed to accept their lot stoically, inured as they were to hard times all their lives. The unrest and violence that broke out in other parts of the country were not in evidence here, but discontent with the apparently helpless Federal Government rose steadily. A few of those taking part in the Bonus March on Washington came through the county but received scant sympathy from the local population, which later quite approved when troops under General MacArthur drove the mobs, turned lawless, out of the capitol city. "We don't hold with that kind of doings", expressed the prevailing opinion.

The drought returned in 1932 and was almost as severe as the earlier one. The suffering was intense, but this was an election year, and a determination built up to turn out an Administration that appeared insensitive to the plight of the common people. The prospect of getting a more effective government in dealing with the Depression gradually lifted public spirits, since it was felt that any change had to be for the better.

Election Day almost seemed like carnival day with the rush to the polls of voters, most of whom were voting emotionally rather than rationally, responding to the promise of a New Deal, even while banks and businesses were failing at an alarming rate. Then came Inauguration Day and, in an area of few radios, everyone who could get to a loudspeaker did so, and listened to the voice, which hypnotized millions for years to come, assure them, "The only thing we have to fear is fear itself". And then the forgotten man went home cheerfully to wait for action to follow the promises.

In the Blue Ridge country, however, he was ill-prepared for the first step toward recovery. On March 6, 1933, a "Banking Holiday" was declared, and the President ordered all banks in the country to be closed until March 15. The effect was shattering. Even though bank accounts might be modest, for most depositors it represented all the financial security they had. To the general run of people, a bank was one of the most stable of institutions a community could have. Now all of a sudden, their doors slammed shut, and people who had money on deposit could not get at it. Fear to the point of panic settled over almost everyone, even though President Roosevelt informed us over the air that this had to be done to get the country straightened out. All that men and women could think of was that to live and to do business to live, one needed money, and now all the money one could spend was what a person had in his pocket and that was precious little. The next nine days were as gloomy as could be. Even after the banks opened again and conditions began to improve, confidence was never fully restored, and the experience left a scar on the soul of the people.

It was not too long before the emergency measures of the New Deal began to manifest themselves. One day, two important looking men with briefcases appeared in Stanardsville and asked help in gathering county officials and leading citizens for a meeting in order to get a Federal relief program started in the county as soon as possible. These turned out to be the forerunners of the W.P.A.—Works Progress Administration—one of the "alphabet soup" agencies spawned by the Roosevelt Administration. According to what we were told, the President and the Congress wanted to get money into the hands of the people as soon as possible, but not in the form of a dole, but through construction programs of every kind for which local persons would be employed. In order that Federal money would not be wasted in the hurried effort to create jobs in the county, it was necessary to appoint a board of responsible, disinterested citizens, acceptable to the people of the county, whose job it would be to supervise the program, to select paid employees to manage the central office, to see to it that worthwhile work projects would be devised to give as many jobs as possible within the limit of the money grants, and to supply the central office in Richmond with all the reports required to expedite the work. They made it clear that all members of the board would be volunteers and that no members of the board could receive pay for any service rendered at any time. Further, they requested especially that the supervisors of the three county districts be appointed to the board. This looked well in theory, but it soon proved to be the source of our worst problems in getting under way.

For such a small county, Greene County was then badly divided politically and between the high land and the low land people. Added to this, local jealousies and interests made it most difficult for the county to function as a unit in the public interest. There were three districts, and the elected supervisors were hostile to each other as they vied for benefits for their tiny domains. As a result, I found myself chosen as chairman of the W.P.A. board by compromise, after a long period of wrangling, as the person most neutral and most to be trusted in the distribution of the Federal goodies. A mountaineer told me: "They picked you for that job, 'cause they thought it was a good chance you wouldn't steal any of the money". Until this matter was settled, no relief projects could get started. The delay irked the Richmond W.P.A. office which phoned almost every day to ask impatiently why we were not working up a program faster and telling us, "Mr. Big says get the money out to the people as quick as you can. So hurry!"

It was a job with no pay and little peace. There wasn't too much difficulty in getting the whole board to vote for such things as repairing and painting the courthouse and landscaping the grounds, improving the jail, working on the public school buildings, and painting the tiny voting booths around the county. But many other projects were badly needed for public benefit as well as to make work for the many unemployed. County roads were in sad condition, new roads to serve isolated areas were a must, and bridges were needed where only fords existed and these were useless at high water. Hundreds of men needed work, but local jealousies put a halt to most plans. The supervisors demanded that projects be awarded to each district as simultaneously and as equally as possible, lest one district would come off better than another. This pulling and tugging seemed senseless in view of the desperate need for jobs, but no one of the three gave ground. The rest of the board preferred to resign rather than override these politicians. The Richmond office was losing patience fast and threatened to take over our operation unless we composed our differences. Loss of tempers kept us from seeing the solution that was obvious.

On re-reading the guidelines given us, it was a surprise to see that it was advisable but not obligatory to have district supervisors as members of the board. They were suggested because of their political influence which might be useful in many localities in securing the cooperation and trust of the people. We had listened well but had done our homework too carelessly under the pressure of getting a program going as soon as possible.

Also, it should have been obvious that the supervisors, who were not men of means, needed paid jobs almost as much as any man in the county, but this was overlooked in the rush. In time, it came out that they felt discriminated against while they helped to plan work to aid others and this had much to do with their attitude. Furthermore, each supervisor would be ideal for recruiting workers and for overseeing projects in his own district where he was known and where he was influential. So after a few quiet conferences, it was suggested at the next board meeting that, while the supervisors might be valuable as members of the board, they were far more needed as field men to push plans through to completion and to see that payrolls were handled properly and accurately. For this they should receive an appropriate salary because their responsibility would be a heavy one, but while they remained members of the hoard, they could not receive compensation. So would they consider resigning and taking over the field work where we needed them so badly? They resigned on the spot.

After that, there were only the irritating little day to day problems arising from self-interest and jealousies. Some property owners pressured us to improve their lanes and drainage ditches, arguing that it would create jobs for poor people. Many farmers abused us for setting a minimum wage of $2.50 a day and so spoiling chances of employing cheap labor. We were accused of favoring special friends and wasting money on dubious work methods such as mending county roads with pick and shovel when mule teams and hand scoops could be rented to do the job far more quickly and cheaply, overlooking the fact that for the time being, we were creating as many jobs as we could and that, as far as we were concerned, busy men were more valuable than the swarms of busybodies which harassed us morning, noon and night.

In due time, the various projects were developed on a large enough scale to be of real use to the public and to get enough money into the hands of the people to relieve their want. Having gotten over the period of real crisis, the Federal planners decided that further programs would be developed on a smaller scale and at a less frenetic pace, since fewer people needed emergency assistance. So the volunteer board was discharged with an official "well done", and a small paid staff took its place, gradually phasing out the venture as the economic condition improved. In spite of all the jibes pointed at the Works Progress Administration; in spite of all the very real mistakes; in spite of all the trivial jobs devised in a hurry; in spite of some boon-doggling; something real and necessary was accomplished. A people plunged deeply into poverty could hope again with full stomachs. The proud mountain people were spared the indignity of living on handouts and were given the chance to earn needed dollars with self-respect. There may not have been a chicken in every pot, but no longer were they compelled to listen helplessly to their children crying with hunger in homes where there was so pitifully little to eat.

Chapter 14

TEMPEST IN A TEAPOT

The Blue Ridge Mountains are particularly lovely in Greene County. They are beautiful along the whole range, but when seen from a favorable location in Stanardsville, the county seat, there is a special grace about them as they rise and fall in the blue haze for which the whole ridge is famous. Looking westward, there is a superb view of the mountains that mark the farthest fringe of the county. On the far left is Flat Top, shaped like a loaf of bread, straddling part of the boundary between Greene and Albemarle. Then rises High Top to a peak filling the skyline between Simmon's Gap and Swift Run Gap, through which the Spotswood Trail runs. To the right of this highway there rises a tumble of mountains—Saddle Back, Lamb's Mountain, the Pocosan—running a northeast line until they vanish from sight in Madison County. This section is a special delight at sunset as the last rays filter through the many gaps in streamers of purple and gold.

For all that it dominates the scene, High Top is less than four thousand feet high, but from its modest height, a goodly portion of Piedmont Virginia to the east and of the Valley of Virginia to the west lies within its view. From a distance, its folds seem gentle with no cliffs and crags visible, giving the whole a kindly appearance. Coming nearer, the roofs of the few little houses that remain shine in the sunlight, marking the scattered abodes of the families sheltered and fed by the mountain.

Along a fifty mile stretch of the Blue Ridge, the long dominant family was Shifflett, clearly of English stock. It is thought that the name

119

was Shiplet originally, suggesting that the ancestors of these mountain folk were once ship-builders. Other families less numerous were mixed in with them along the range. For example, in this hollow, the families were Shiffletts and Morrises. On that mountain, were Shiffletts and Breedens. And so it went from place to place: Shiffletts and Knights; Shiffletts and Sullivans; Shiffletts and Lambs, with sprinklings of Taylors, Colliers, and Roaches, along with many others. Up to two generations ago, representatives of most of these families nestled at one time or another on the slopes and in the dips of High Top like children in the lap of an ample primeval nurse, but most are gone now.

This mountain, like all the Blue Ridge, is what the geologists call "an erosional remnant". It is capped by a hard, greenish rock, named Catoctin schist, once forced up in molten form from the fiery furnaces deep below the surface of the land. It resists erosion and so supports a range, which is all that is left of an escarpment forming the western edge of a plateau now nearly worn away by the waters of millions of years. This hard material breaks down slowly, creating a thin but fertile layer of earth, which produces splendid pastures of blue grass for cattle and good crops for people where it can be farmed.

The face of High Top presents many contrasts. Some areas are not worth clearing because of slopes too steep for cultivation and extensive outcroppings of stone. Not even good for pasture, these sections were allowed to be taken over by woods, which supplied ample fuel for heating and cooking. On the Western side, the open land supported many herds. There was no lack of water, except in extreme droughts. Abundant, high yield springs copiously supplied the needs of the people and of their animals.

Portions of several of the little farms presented an unbelievable sight. Acres were covered by rocks of all sizes and sharp boulders sticking up out of the ground like asparagus spears, yet they were under cultivation. Little soil was visible, and nothing could look more worthless. When the Federal Government sent out officials to settle the claims of the mountaineers, whose land had been condemned for the Shenandoah National Park, these worthies could see no value in those stony fields. So they felt that they were more than generous in offering the owners five dollars an acre. They were shocked when the offer was angrily refused and assumed that the mountain folk were trying to gouge the

Government without a glimmer of conscience. This caused delay and litigation before the matter was settled.

What the harried officials did not know at first was that such wretched looking land was ideal for farming and that it produced very good corn crops. Because a field could not be plowed, it did not follow that it could not support people. Between the rocks and boulders were irregular strips of soil four to six inches wide. When corn planting season came for the highland farmer, the whole family was mobilized for work, and, if time was pressing, neighbors would lend a hand and expect help in their turn.

All kinds of useful containers would have been gathered in advance, such as pails, tubs, sacks and boxes. Also in advance, soil would have been hauled up to the planting area by wagons or mountain sleds and piled up for use. When all was ready, two or three men appointed as droppers would sling on canvas bags of seed corn and start out in roughly parallel lines suitably spaced, dropping the kernels between the rocks and boulders. Behind them would come any extra men, the women and the children, all carrying earth in any container that each could manage and covering the seed to a proper depth.

It was hard work but worth it, because when the job was finished, it was really finished. There was no hoeing or plowing to be done. Some weeds would have to be pulled at times, but little else would be needed until harvest except to watch the corn grow in the rich dirt to a height that would command the respect of a Kansas farmer. Little wonder that the mountaineer rejected the offer of five dollars an acre with a sense of utter outrage.

Now most of High Top lies within the boundaries of the Shenandoah National Park, and few of its people remain. Four decades ago the population was considerable by mountain standards, and living conditions were austere with few advantages. The only center of community activity was a dreary, unpainted one room schoolhouse. Cracks around the ill-fitting windows and some broken window panes, mended by cardboard, let in the winter cold with which the sheet-iron wood stove could scarcely contend. In other seasons, the building provoked little complaint from people who had few comforts.

The interior was simply furnished with desks, tables, seats, and blackboards sufficient for the school and for the few meetings held only in daylight hours, because no electric line had yet been run up the mountain. Pupils of all ages were under the supervision of an elderly male school teacher on whom the people looked as their adviser and authority in all cultural and intellectual matters.

There was no church and no resident minister of any denomination on High Top. Visiting preachers held occasional services in the schoolhouse and so did local self-ordained farmers, who felt called on to preach, but there was no regular pastor to look after the people. Several times during my first three years I worked in Greene County I had been asked by many of the people to come up at least twice a month and hold services. At the time, I had six missions to look after and could not consider accepting the invitation, especially as the trip would be rugged and would take more time on Sundays than I could spare. Later, however, I was given an assistant, who relieved me of the care of three missions, thus allowing me to schedule regular services for the High Top folk.

There were certain difficulties connected with this venture. The first problem to solve was how to get up the mountain by automobile and then safely down. The few roads on both sides were called so only by extravagant courtesy. It was soon obvious that one could not advisedly return by the way he went up. Nor could he drive up by the way he was to come down, because the road was so steep and rough that no automobile of that era had the power to make the grade.

To get to the schoolhouse, one had to drive west over the Swift Run Gap to Elkton, then turn south to Yancey and take the dirt road leading steeply up the mountain. That was only the start because there were twelve pasture gates to open and close before reaching the schoolhouse, and that was a tedious chore. Then, too, by midday the cattle were moving around actively, and the lively ones would often race me for the open gates when I went down by the way I came up. This added problem was a little too much to cope with and ruled out the west road as a return route. So the matter settled itself. It had to be up from the Shenandoah Valley by way of Yancey, down the western slope to Haneytown, and then east out to Stanardsville. The descent by car was enough to sober anyone—rocky and steep. The people advised, "Better tie some bresh to your car to slow you down". However, low gear and the foot brake were dependable enough, if one took it easy.

Another difficulty was the fact that the High Top people had a very strong religious bent, demanding "preaching from the Bible" and sermons seasoned with brimstone and whiffs from the abode of the damned. In their drab life, they responded to emotional appeals, and a good pulpit thumping preacher was more acceptable than one who had a "come now and let us reason together" approach. Semi-illiterate though they were, many had a remarkable knowledge of the Bible from "spelling it out", and also held to a rigid orthodoxy of the Fundamentalist type. They indulged freely in religious arguments and supported their views by loud declarations, "It's in the Book".

Among them were a few who undertook to preach from time to time but not as a profession. These had some local following, even though their pulpiteering had more "whoop-'em-up" than substance. These tended to look on visiting clergy with a suspicious eye, especially those who seemed to have more education than was good for the soul, and were alert to detect departures from sound doctrine according to their lights. Anything that sounded new or different was sure to be of the devil, and any stranger who came up on the mountain was eyed doubtfully as an exponent of the faith until he had been certified as "sound" by the local panel of spiritual watchdogs.

The first trip to begin the schedule was on a lovely Sunday early in May. However, the beauty of the weather and the scenery was dulled for the time being by the monotonous routine of the dreary passage of the twelve gates, repeated over and over. The procedure was this: drive up to the first gate as near as convenient, depending upon which way the gate swung; put on the emergency brake; get out of the car; chock the back wheels (there were plenty of large stones round); open the gate; get back into the car; release the brake slowly; drive through; stop the car; put on the brake; get out; chock the back wheels; close the gate; get back into the car; release the brake slowly; drive on to the next gate and repeat the operation eleven more times. The tedium was relieved only by the necessity of chasing cows, now and then, away from a gate far enough to allow getting the car through without having any cattle escape. The first trip was the worst; after that, one ran the obstacle course as a matter of course,

Getting to the schoolhouse finally, there was no one in sight. This aroused the worry that word of the service had not been spread around but, remembering that in some places in the mountains the people take their time coming to meetings, there was no cause for concern yet. Few had clocks or watches anyway. Most went by the sun and estimates of time varied widely. Since there was no hurry and since the schoolhouse was locked, I had ample time to look around and enjoy the scenery. The sky was clear, there was little haze, and visibility was of a rare quality in all directions. To the west one could see clearly the youthful Alleghenies. In sight were long stretches of the Shenandoah Valley and also the sweep of the hills rolling down from the Blue Ridge to the east.

As it turned out, the wait was not long, for presently a middle-aged man and his wife appeared walking along a path, which came up over a steep rise. After introductions, the husband excused himself and went to unlock the little building and to kindle a fire in the stove because the spring weather at that height was rather chilly. Conversation with his wife was not easy. Like all mountain people, she was diffident in the presence of an outlander. After trying two or three subjects with little success, I commented on the landscape:

"You all certainly have a wonderful view from up here. I haven't seen many places with a better one. You people are mighty fortunate."

"Lord have mercy", she replied, "I don't see nothing pretty about these old ugly, rocky hills. You have to work so hard and git so tired jest to keep alive scrabbling a living from these here stones. You git old while you are young up here. We never see a good time. Spring, summer, and fall, it's all work, work, work. In winter, folks stay close to the fire trying to keep life in the body. Ain't nothing to do except maybe git in trouble, and we got too much of that the way I see it."

I tried to change the mood by calling her attention to the clouds of dogwood blossoms spreading out in all directions below, splashed with scarlet here and there, where the Judas trees bloomed, saying:

"Few people ever see such a thrilling sight like that!"

"Yes," she agreed, but pointed toward neighboring mountain slopes, where grey areas scarred the bright, soft, spring green of the woods. "Look over there at those dead'nings. I remember when big chestnut trees stood tall and straight in place of those dead trunks. We used to git a passel of chestnuts every year, but I ain't tasted none for a long time. I hear tell that some sickness is killing chestnuts all over the country. 'Course, men git some money cutting them and hauling the logs out

124

to the sawmill. They sell the bark for tanning, but it is all ugly now where the pretty trees used to grow—ugly like everything else up here. I hate it."

With that, she kicked a small stone and sent it spinning.

"If life is all that bad up here, why do you and your husband stay?" I asked.

"Jest for one reason", she replied. "We don't know nothing else. We were born and raised here. Bad as it seems, I don't believe we could stand living somewhars out yonder. It's all the home we got, so we try to do the best we kin."

By this time, a goodly number of people had gathered, and the ad hoc sexton announced that the building was ready. So after shaking hands all around, we went in and had a very informal service, since few of them had even heard of the Book of Common Prayer. That could wait. The singing of gospel hymns was a cappella and the prayers impromptu. After a lesson from the Authorized, or King James Version of the Bible, I preached without notes somewhat in the style they expected. To have used notes would have been a disaster from the outset, for in their opinion any preacher who preached from paper instead of "from the heart" was no preacher at all.

The service went off without untoward incident. I noticed, however, that the local evangelist observed me quite closely and even looked up the biblical references I used in the Bible, which he habitually carried around with him. Also, I noticed that some of the people watched him as much as they watched me to try to discover whether or not their primus inter pares was going to give the new minister "a good name".

After that, all went well for several services and I assumed that I was well enough established to introduce the use of the Book of Common Prayer, which was accepted in other mountain areas, partly because the language and style were not strange to them. So I borrowed a number of spare copies from Grace Church, Stanardsville, and took them with me to the next meeting. I was ill prepared for the tempest in a teapot that followed.

We started as usual with a hymn and an extempore prayer. Then I distributed the service books and requested the people to turn to Psalm 1 and read it responsively with me. All cooperated except the dean of the mountain, who ostentatiously opened his copy of the Authorized

Version of the Bible and tried to follow the Psalm from that translation. It didn't work. Psalm I in the Book of Common Prayer is Archbishop Cranmer's translation. After a verse or two, he closed his Bible, sat down, folded his arms, and stared moodily out of the window. The Psalm finished, I read a lesson from the Scriptures and started to deliver the sermon. In a moment, I was interrupted by a shout:

"Hold on thar, you! You ain't doing right" It was the lay preacher, red of face and eyes blazing. The congregation began to stir nervously, for it was not uncommon for services to be broken up by dissension.

"What am I doing wrong?" I asked.

"You are using the wrong Bible," he accused.

"There is no wrong Bible!" I contended.

"Oh, yes, there is and you got it! This is the right Bible, the one I learned the Word of God from, and you got no business coming up here and reading out of the wrong book, which ain't like this one," he roared, holding up his blue cloth covered Bible and slapping it again and again for emphasis.

I tried to calm him down by explaining that the Old Testament was written in Hebrew and the New Testament in Greek, not English; that the Bible had been translated many times in many languages; and that most translations differed in form but not in content, so there was no wrong Bible. I offered some examples but he kept shaking his head from side to side.

When I paused, he returned to the attack with increased bitterness: "You got the wrong Bible, mister, and that's all thar is to it. I hear what you got to say. It don't make no sense, and you got nothing to prove it. Look here, you know what the Bible says about you?" he asked shaking his finger at me.

"Lots of things, I am sure, but I don't know what you have in mind. The Bible is a big book", I answered.

"I'll tell you. Right here it's written as plain as day in the Book, in the last chapter of Revelation,

> 'I testify unto every man that heareth the words of the
> prophecy of this book, if any man shall add unto these
> things, God shall add unto him the plagues that are
> written in this book: and if any man shall take away
> from the words of the book of this prophecy, God shall
> take away his part out of the book of life, and out of

the holy city, and from the things which are written in this book.'

"That's what it says", he declared. "So you better look out, mister, or you'll be damned."

He sat down, breathing hard. Looking around, it was evident that I was losing ground with the congregation. Anyway, we had reached a dead end for the moment, so I suggested to my opponent that we call a temporary truce, saying,

"You don't know what I am talking about and I don't know what you are talking about. We are too excited now to do the Lord or the people much good. We need time to cool off, so let's stop right here. The next time I come up, I'll bring up some of the books I have been talking about so that you and the folks here can see them and maybe we can settle this business to suit us all, because we are all Christians."

I turned to the congregation and asked, "Do you think that this is fair?" To my relief, they all nodded their heads—all except my grim faced adversary. Then I dismissed the congregation and drove the long way home.

There was plenty of time the next two weeks to think the matter over, and I felt sure that I had to recover lost ground if I planned to keep on going up on High Top. Some reports of the encounter had percolated down to the village, and friends informed me sympathetically that my opponent had prided himself on having "run more than one no account preacher off the mountain". So I collected the items that I thought I could use to advantage: three versions of the Bible in English; the New Testament in Greek; the Old Testament in Greek (the Septuagint); the whole Bible in Portuguese; and the New Testament in German, which latter I took along for show only as I had not yet learned to read German.

On the next scheduled Sunday, I got up much earlier than usual; hurried through the quick breakfast my patient wife prepared; stowed the needed materials in the car; and took off in order to have over an hour alone in the schoolhouse before the congregation assembled, since by now I had been entrusted with a key. Arriving, it was a relief to see that no one was around and that preparations could be made without interruptions.

The schoolhouse was provided with five large black-boards and plenty of chalk. Taking the first verse of the first Psalm, which triggered the controversy, I chalked up three different versions in English; one in Greek; and one in Portuguese. Taking the first word in the Psalm, "Blessed", I wrote under it seven different ways in which it could be rendered. Afterward, there was time to write the opening words of a couple of well known and loved texts from the New Testament and to give different translations of each. The whole made an impressive showing when finished, but I felt a measure of self-reproach for over-doing it which dissipated when I saw the effect it had on the people when the congregation began to gather.

Word had evidently gotten around that there would be "big doings" at the schoolhouse that morning, because there was standing room only in the little structure when everybody had entered for the opening hymn. The singing was rather ragged for attention was fixed on the blackboards and whispering interfered with praise. The schoolmaster was present and two or three other teachers from the nearby low country. Also a couple of men who looked like they might be preachers, ordained or lay, sat with the local evangelist. At the beginning, the mood seemed to be that I should be given a fair chance.

When the time came for the address, instinct and experience dictated that the matter should be handled coolly and kindly, avoiding any touch of polemics. I spoke of the distress I felt that my gospel friend and I were so unfortunate as to have had a serious difference due to misunderstanding only, seeing that we shared the same faith. Then I told the congregation how glad I was to be given the opportunity now to explain more clearly what I meant by different translations, seeing that on my last visit I did not have the books with me to make my point plain.

Picking up the different versions of the Bible, I described each one briefly and laid them open on a table, inviting the people to look at them all they wanted after the service. Then some time was spent with the material on the blackboards, showing how the Scriptures could be rendered in many ways and in many tongues, without hurting the truth of the Bible, as the examples showed so plainly. It was very heartening to observe that the congregation paid close attention and also that the schoolmaster nodded his head in agreement several times. I volunteered to answer any questions after the service and ventured the hope that the air now had been cleared and that I and those who had taken issue with me could be friends again.

Right after the closing hymn, the schoolmaster went immediately to the table and became greatly interested in the Greek version of the Old Testament, turning the pages of a short section one by one. This was such a good omen that I did not even hint that he was holding the book upside down. I retired to the door while many of those present went up to look at the books and to discuss them with the teachers. As the people left, they shook hands cordially and said that they would see me the next time. This meant that, as far as they were concerned, the crisis was over.

Best of all, my challenger came out to shake hands and to introduce his friends as though nothing had happened. It was obvious that what had happened the former Sunday was to be ignored from now on. To show his goodwill, he insisted that I come to eat dinner with him and his family the next time I was on the mountain.

This I did and had a good visit and meal with pleasant conversation. Afterward, he showed me around his well kept modest farm, of which he was quite proud. My strongest recollection of the visit was the large tract of land covered thickly with rocks and boulders with sprouts of new corn peeping up between them, as though symbolizing the fact that there was more to this mountain and its people than a superficial observer would ever know.

Chapter 15

ASHES TO ASHES

One morning, not long after I had taken up work in Greene County in 1930, I received word that a seventeen year old boy had been killed accidentally by mishandling a shotgun, and I was asked to come up on Lamb's Mountain the next day at two o'clock to "preach the funeral". The messenger, a kinsman, was vague on details except to say that the family was "taking it hard" and that the funeral was to be in the family graveyard. He did tell that, to reach it, I should drive as far as I could up the mountain road, then park the car, take the path on the right and walk maybe half a mile. Since I was scheduled for another funeral in a few hours, there was no time to visit the bereaved family beforehand.

The next day, allowing plenty of time, I drove up the mountain and, after parking, I made my way with my vestments toward the burial plot as directed. I arrived just as the mission worker was concluding the Burial Office. While I was recovering from my surprise, my arrival was noted. The grave was still open, and the family and friends were standing around the excavation. Many of the women were grieving loudly. The father of the deceased walked over to me at once and said, "It got so late that we didn't think that you was a-coming, so I asked the mission lady to do the burying. We'd a-waited some if we knowed you was on the way."

At that moment, his wife joined us. She was emotionally overwrought, and I tried to comfort her but without success. Presently, she became calmer and I asked her if there was anything I could do. She nodded vigorously and said, "I wished and wished for you to git here. The lady done all right but it ain't fitting for a body to be buried without preaching. The praying is over, but we are all here yit. My boy was a good boy, and I want things done right for him. I want you to preach a sermon over him right now!"

So I stood at the head of the grave and did the best I could, sharing with all present the comfort and hope we have in the Risen Christ, and finished with a benediction. Then I signaled to the men, who were standing by with shovels, to begin filling the grave. Perhaps there is no sound so desolating as the sound of the "ca-lump" of the first shovel of earth as it strikes the lid of the wooden box containing the coffin. At that, the wailing broke out afresh and continued until the job was finished, the grave properly mounded over, and suitable stones placed at the head and the foot. Then the group of family and friends broke up and each started for home.

The mountain people were and still are stern realists and face the stark events of life without evasion. At death, there is no effort to pretend that what has happened has not happened. There are no plastic carpets of fake grass to cover the piled up dirt or to soften the raw edges of the grave. At the words "ashes to ashes, dust to dust", plain earth, not flower petals nor rosebuds, is sprinkled on the casket. The family does not retire some supposedly kind distance, while the pall bearers do their work with shovel and spade. The bereaved stay with their dead until all things necessary are completed and then take up life's routine again with stoic acceptance of their loss.

I was glad that I could render some service, but I was distinctly annoyed that the funeral was held ahead of time, as my watch showed that I was at least fifteen minutes early. Quickly, I discovered that my initiation into the mountain ways was not complete. On the Pocosans, Saddle Back and Lamb's Mountain at least, the time was not Eastern Standard but their own time, which here was more than an hour ahead of my time. No one had taken the trouble to enlighten me on this point.

There were no radios. The availability and use of that wonder was yet several years away. There was only one telephone in the area, and apparently no one had ever thought of using the instrument to find out what time it was. The sun governed the people's day, and finickiness with regard to the hour or minute was important only to those who had nothing better to do. Those who had no watches and clocks were content with approximate time, and no two time pieces ever agreed. The schedule was a simple one. Except for Sundays, they worked hard from sun-up to sun-down and, after the evening meal, fell exhausted into bed.

It might be thought that the mission workers, better educated and more sophisticated, would have used their influence to improve this situation, or at least would have kept their watches and clocks on time. Some did and some didn't. Those who did not were usually the veterans, who had spent long years in isolated stations. Weeks and months passed with a numbing sameness, and boredom brought relaxation of a scheduled way of life and work. Thus, they tended to function on the time of the people whom they served, regardless of complications.

As much as this experience taught me, school was not yet out. About a year later, I was called on to hold a funeral service at Upper Pocosan. Again the hour was set for two o'clock. It was January and the weather was bad in the lowlands but bitter up on the mountains which were covered with snow and ice. I allowed considerable time over what was usually needed to make the trip, in order to take care of possible problems caused by the weather and the common disdain for Eastern Standard Time. My wife came with me to drive the car when I would inevitably have to get out and push, or fill bad ruts with stones, or shovel gravel on slick places in order to get traction.

We made it by the hardest as far as the Lower Pocosan Mission without too much delay. But beyond the mission, just below George Lamb's home and farm, the road was blocked by snowdrifts, and there was no possibility of getting through. We managed to back out of trouble, turn around, and drive back to the mission where I left my wife and the automobile, and then set out to walk the three miles to Upper Pocosan. It was uphill all the way and that day it was rough going every foot on account of deep snow and the many wind-swept places where the road was covered with ice. The trip was made worse by time pressure, which allowed scant opportunity for rest pauses.

After what seemed an eternity, I reached a spot at a bend in the road about a quarter of a mile from the cemetery where I was compelled to stop and catch my breath. In a moment, around the bend came the vanguard of a stream of people toward me, and I learned that once more

I was a victim of the time chaos. I was told this time that I was two hours late and the people could wait no longer, so they got the mission lady to hold the service. It is well to skip over what passed between me and the mission lady. With the people all I could do was to show them my watch, which did not help at all because the mountain patriarch was present. He had a watch which did not agree with mine at all. From the silent nods exchanged among the people, it was plain that I was the loser as to principle but I did have the sympathy of all for having to make such a trip for nothing.

So back down the road I went, having the company of some of the people part way, which helped. With a bitter cold wind at my back, the walk down to Lower Pocosan was fairly speedy. There, to my undying gratitude, I found that the two mission workers and my wife had a good hot meal ready for me, and never had rest and refreshment been so welcome. On the way back home, a resolution was formed and firmed up not to take anything for granted again, especially where people living back in the far reaches of the mountains were concerned. Thereafter, when I was requested to come out for any function at a particular time, I always asked, "What time is your time?"

Reference has been made twice with regard to two o'clock being set as the time for a funeral. It was customary to bury the dead in the afternoon between the hours of two and four, because it used to be considered unlucky to leave a grave open overnight. There were practical reasons as well as superstition for it. Grave diggers were not professionals, but they were men recruited from family and friends for whom it was more convenient to do their work the day of the funeral. Then too, a pre-dug grave might fill with water after a hard rain, and this would cause much extra labor and delay. Also, livestock wandering around at night might fall into the excavation.

Usually, the grave was dug the morning of the burial. This did not always work out well. Often the diggers would run into rock, or large tree roots, or loose gravel that had to be shored up with boards. In winter, frozen ground was a problem also. More often than not, the service would have to be delayed while the grave was being finished, and that meant a wait of an hour or more. Then the casket would be placed on the ground to one side, while the people stood or sat where they were out of the way. The wait was usually spent in quiet conversation and, if the delay was going to be long, the men and some of the women would take out their pipes for a leisurely smoke.

Few cemeteries in the mountains were at or near a church. Most of them were family plots on the old home place, and few could be reached by automobile, so rough was the terrain. Good, much needed land was not generally set aside for burial grounds. A few decades ago morticians and hearses were seldom seen in the hills. A casket, or a box serving as a casket, was often made locally. When one was purchased from an undertaker at the courthouse, he would bring it out to the foot of the ridge by truck. From there, it would be hauled up the mountain by wagon to the home of the deceased, who had been prepared for interment, which was usually the next day. Such preparation was simple, especially in the days when few bodies were embalmed. Burial followed death as soon as decently possible.

However, the activities after a death could be hectic. In the past, there were certain proprieties and even superstitions to be complied with. Time was, and not too long ago, when at a death all mirrors would be turned to the wall, all pictures covered with cloths, and all clocks stopped if there were any in the home. No one seemed to be able to explain the practice except to say that it was an old custom. At the bottom of it seemed to be an old superstition, namely, when life ends, it is urgent that a person's soul should go at once to its resting place. The ticking of a clock might distract it, delay its journey, and cause it to lose its way into the beyond. Thus, the disembodied spirit would linger restlessly and distressfully in the locality, possibly causing undesirable and scary things to happen. Similarly, a reflecting surface, like a framed picture or mirror, was apt to catch and imprison the departing haunt, holding it within the house, which was good for neither the living nor the dead.

Regardless of what might or might not be done first, the important thing was for the women to make ready for the influx of visitors, who would start coming soon to comfort the family and pay their respects, while the men attended to details of the funeral. From then on, every able-bodied member of the family would be kept mercifully busy. House and grounds would be tidied up. Food and drink would be prepared for callers, many of whom would have come from a distance and would probably stay for the all night wake. There would be little rest for anybody, for in time of trouble, mountain folk rallied around for support as long as they felt that they would be needed, which meant until after the funeral. Cooking and dishwashing, along with other duties, were almost endless.

In the meantime, the casket, when ready for display, was placed in the best and most accessible part of the house, and the lid was propped open so that all who wished might view the body. It remained open until the time came to take it to a church or directly to the place of burial. If taken to the church for the service, it was the custom to open the coffin again following the benediction or hymn, and perhaps again at the graveside, no matter what the condition of the body or cause of death might be. If there was to be no service at a church, almost certainly the coffin would be opened at the cemetery for "a last look". This custom was most trying, for it was usually the signal for the female kin to set up a loud weeping and wailing, which emotionally upset most of those present. It has been most difficult to break up this practice because of public opinion which demanded two things: that proper respect should be shown for the dead and that the bereaved "take it hard".

Families were deeply attached sentimentally to their family burial plots, even though they did not keep them in very good condition. Most of these plots had one thing in common: it took heroic measures to bury the dead in them, quite apart from the labor of digging a grave in such poor soil. To repeat, many burial plots were located on ground not fit for anything else and not a few were virtually inaccessible. It required the virtual mobilization of the able-bodied men of the area to get the coffin to the place of interment.

The last funeral I held in the South River section is illustrative. On this occasion there was no time problem, nor premature starting; only the problem of getting there. It was March and it did not seem too cold with a bright sun doing its best to temper the cold wind sweeping down the mountain. The time set was the usual two o'clock on a Thursday afternoon. The burial ground was on a spur above South River and about a mile from Lower Pocosan Mission. I was notified that the casket, followed by the mourners, would be brought up by a path, which was winding and difficult to travel, above the mission. However, I was advised not to take that route but to park my car at the mission and then walk by the "nigh way" to the cemetery which I could not miss even though the path at times seemed to carry me away from my destination. Also, I was told that a small stream crossed the path at a dip on its way to join South River, but that I should have no trouble getting across it.

When the time came, I followed instructions to the letter until I got to the stream and there found that the situation did not fit the description. The water was high because of the run-off from melting snow on the mountain. Above and below the ford, the deep narrow channel was a foaming turmoil of icy water. At the ford, the channel widened out and the water seemed shallower, but the stepping stones I was told were there were out of sight under the little flood. A short walk up and then down the stream made it clear that the only possible way across was at the ford, and the passage would be a wet one. I cut a small pole and made soundings. As far as I could make out, the water was nearly hip deep. It looked and felt dishearteningly cold. If I was going to get to that funeral on time, I would have to wade.

Above the ford, the stream was quite narrow, and the ground on the far side was dry and clear of underbrush. First, I threw my overcoat and suit coat across. Looking around carefully in all directions, the place seemed deserted. So off came my shoes and socks and they were thrown over. In a moment, my nether garments joined them. It was cold where I was but the water looked colder. It was no time to hesitate, so I started wading across at the ford with my vestment case held high. Fortunately, my estimate proved correct, and I got over without mishap, though the hidden slippery stones were something of a problem.

Once over, I felt almost paralyzed from wet skin exposed to the stiff wind. Drying off as best I could with handkerchiefs and a muffler, I was soon garbed and hiked rapidly up the trail to make up for lost time and to work up circulation. When I got to the burial ground, my teeth had stopped chattering, and I found that I had arrived ahead of the casket and the people. Looking down the slope to the east, I could see the procession about a quarter of a mile away moving slowly and with difficulty.

Mention has been made that it often took heroic measures to bury the dead in many family plots. This funeral was certainly a case in point. The path was narrow, rough, winding now down and now up-grade with scarcely a level spot anywhere. The coffin was heavy and in this location could only be moved by manpower. The method used was to pass three ropes, evenly spaced, under the coffin. Then three pairs of men would take corresponding places on either side; stoop and loop the ropes over their shoulders, thus making a kind of sling; rise together and try to move forward in step until exhausted. Underbrush on both sides of the path, in places head high, made concerted action difficult and the task more burdensome.

When the first group could go no further, a second squad of six would take its place, and so on until the little cemetery was reached. In this case, there were over twenty men, all volunteers, to perform this service. Thus, three interchangeable groups moved the coffin along in hitches. There were a few substitutes, because at times the coffin would twist and swing erratically, due to the poor terrain, and a rope might easily slip and put a pall bearer out of action with a bad skin burn. It frequently happened.

However, the journey was completed without mishap, and the extremely weary young men sat down to rest after lowering the casket into the grave. The remaining tasks were taken over by the older men. Anon, the service was held, the grave filled in, and large stones were placed at the head and foot. Then the assemblage slowly disbanded, and the people went their separate ways. Needless to say, I walked back the "fur way", having had my fill of the "nigh way".

Chapter 16

A SUNDAY AFTERNOON OUTING

As one from the more sophisticated lowlands, where a large percentage of church members tends to be rather casual about attendance on services, I never ceased to be surprised and pleased by the comparatively large congregations at most of my six mountain chapels. Quite impressive was the fact that nearly all the people walked, and distances varied from a few hundred yards to as much as four miles up and down steep roads and rough trails. Whole families would turn out when the weather was favorable. Babies were carried by their parents. Generally there was one, and the father and the mother took turns toting it. If there were two small ones, each took charge of one. That meant slow travelling since there had to be frequent stops for rest. The older children would scamper on ahead of the elders, playing with one another and with other children as they met them along the way. The teen-agers scorned to be seen with the small fry and sought the company of their own kind; boys gathering with boys, and girls with girls, as mixing of the sexes above the age of puberty was frowned upon in those days by the culture of which they were a part.

Church goers aimed to arrive early to make it worthwhile expending so much effort. The adults not only wanted to have time to rest but plenty of opportunity to visit and to gossip with friends and kin. Men gathered with men and women with women on the church grounds, and the young sorted themselves out in customary groups. Two generations ago this constituted the main social activity of the week, and all ages looked forward to it. The better part of Sundays was dedicated to companionship along with worship. Socializing went on after the service as well as before. The only time limit set was that all should plan to get home before dark. The mountaineers were not at all concerned about the length of the service or the sermon. They had plenty of time, and, after all, what had they come for? They were critical of short sermons anyway, holding that brief homilies indicated that the preacher wasn't converted enough to exhort sinners properly.

The most typical of my missions was the one up on Saddle Back Mountain, whose congregation numbered well over a hundred and took in most of the people living on its eastern slopes. The chapel was in reality a multi-purpose building. Services were held there on Sundays. During the week it became a school, except in summer time. When the need arose, it served as an auditorium for community meetings. The building was far from impressive to look at since it was a weather-beaten structure, which was seldom painted, though kept in good repair. It held the congregation comfortably, but there was little room to spare.

In the winter, the chapel was heated unevenly by a wood stove, which the men tended faithfully and for which they kept an ample supply of wood cut and stacked against the south outside wall. When the fire died down, the building cooled off quickly as the walls and ceiling were not insulated. A man sitting close by would then open the top of the stove noisily, chunk up the fire, throw more wood in, and close the lid with a bang. In a few moments, the heat would become oppressive. Then the only door would be opened to cool things off, with the result that people sitting near the little chancel would feel too hot and the people on the back pews would suffer from the chill wind, there being no storm door to protect them. A good deal of time on freezing Sundays would be taken up in the nave by animated whispered conversations about regulating the temperature, while the minister carried on as best he could.

In the summer time, comfort problems were still difficult but more easily solved. The roof was of tin with plank sheathing underneath for support and no insulation at all. In clear weather, the sun beat unmercifully upon the metal and drove the congregation outside. A stone memorial altar had been built close by for such a contingency, and it was situated charmingly in a grove of oak trees. There wasn't a sprig of grass, but the ground was covered with gravel and with rocks from egg size to large boulders. The latter served to seat the worshippers whose requirements for comfort were very modest indeed.

Though the building was little better than a shack and the furnishings sparse and rustic, it was a homelike place to hold a service once the congregation was inside, provided that the minister was not bothered by the conditions under which he had to function and which the people accepted as normal. From time to time babies became cross and restless. Their crying made speaking difficult until their mothers breast fed them and petted them to sleep. It was openly done and no one except visitors from the outside saw anything unusual about the procedure. It was rather cozy to have a couple of small children playing along the communion rail and a dog in the tiny chancel sleeping beside the lectern. The only problem was to take care not to step on any of them in moving around. Excepting the few times when fights occurred, the atmosphere of the place was easy and relaxed.

It was not easy, however, to get used to the parading of men and boys in and out of the service while I was officiating. Down the gentle slope below the building in a protected spot was an excellent spring with a copious flow of water, which was wonderfully cool, even in the hottest weather. It was to this spring that the restless males repaired when they walked out. For them it was a kind of a 'time out' of short duration to get a drink or to catch a quick smoke and then stroll back leisurely to the service. In summer this movement caused little disturbance. However, during the winter months, in the small crowded chapel, it was a problem since the congregation in the back was chilled with each opening and closing of the door.

This nuisance, though, was trivial compared to the ever-present possibility of serious trouble among the young men, who tended to be high spirited and easily offended. Most were well behaved, but at times a few would arrive charged up with "white lightning" and in quarrelsome moods. It was up to the minister to watch for trouble and head it off when signs appeared, since he had the responsibility of keeping the peace. This put a bit of a strain on him because it was not a simple matter to separate in his mind the youngsters who had come to church because they wanted to, from those who had come simply for the reason that there was nothing else going on around the mountain and they were bored with hanging around home. The latter were the potential trouble makers.

A case in point was provided by one of them on a cold winter Sunday afternoon. His Bible reading mother had named him Titus. He had reached the age when he felt that it was necessary to demonstrate his manhood and independence on suitable occasions to impress his family and peers. This afternoon, Titus lagged behind when his family started off for church as soon as dinner was over. He really did not want to go to church, but neither did he want to be alone. Anon, he put on his cap and overcoat and ambled leisurely down the road, bothered not one whit by the fact that he would be late for the service that I was conducting. After walking about half a mile, he detoured by a place that he often frequented when he had some money, and purchased what he considered an adequate supply of moonshine to protect him against the cold. By the time he neared the chapel, the level in the bottle had lowered considerably, and Titus was experiencing a rosy glow. Knowing that it was not advisable to arrive at the mission with a conspicuous bulge in his overcoat pocket, he stopped to consider the problem.

Ahead, the road made a bend around a small patch of woods and then went straight down past the chapel in full sight of anyone on the premises. Just at the bend, there was a pile of stones for road repair. His glance fell on it and, in his rather hazy state, he imagined that right here he could protect his investment and at the same time avoid unwelcome observation. So he made a space in the pile, placed the half-empty bottle in the hole, covered it with rocks, and then walked on feeling that his cache was safe, not knowing that he had grievously miscalculated.

In the back pew, on the right side of the chapel, sat three of Titus' acquaintances and contemporaries. The one next to the window had rather lost interest in the service and was glancing outside just at the time Titus was engaged in his security measures. At the distance it was not possible to see precisely what Titus was doing, but it looked interesting and worth investigating at a propitious moment. He watched Titus pick his way carefully and judged that he had good reason to be unsteady as he approached the chapel entrance. Titus stumbled a bit on the steps and then paused to regain his balance while he held the door open, much to the annoyance of the worshippers. Then he closed the door noisily and chose a seat near the stove. Having come in from the cold, Titus relaxed pleasantly in the welcome warmth. In a few minutes drowsiness overcame him and he fell fast asleep. The friend, who was watching him closely, judged that the propitious moment had arrived. He reached for his hat and overcoat and whispered to the other two, "Let's go to the spring". So they slipped out much to the disgruntlement of some seated in the back pews, who took exception to so much coming and going with the alternate waves of warmth and gusts of cold.

Once at the spring, the two puzzled friends were quickly brought up to date, and they agreed that the rock pile should be investigated immediately, since there was no telling how long Titus would be asleep, and since Titus' notoriously bad temper would be difficult to cope with if he caught them. The three then went down below the spring far enough to be out of sight of anyone in the chapel and then cut up to the patch of woods and made for the rock pile. In a moment the bottle was found, the contents quickly consumed and the empty reburied. Then the trio returned to the chapel by way of the spring, and settled back into their vacated pew. To their relief, they saw that Titus was still sound asleep and remained that way until the service was drawing to a close. Then, Titus roused up, got his cap and overcoat, and made his way out through the door under the cross glares of worshippers tiring by now of so much traffic. Oblivious to such adverse public opinion, Titus headed in a roundabout way to the rock pile with no reason to suspect that all was not well.

In the meantime, I had taken note of the activity but had seen nothing to cause undue alarm, even though it was more than annoying. Not until a few days later did I find out what had been going on, though I wondered a bit at the time, not knowing that soon I would have enough to contend with.

Shortly after Titus' departure, I concluded the service and during the closing hymn I went behind the organ; removed my vestments, there being no vesting room in the tiny building; and got ready to leave while the last hymn was being sung. At the "Amen", a few of the congregation started out of the door. Suddenly, there was a thud, something struck the side of the building. It was followed by a bang, when an object bounced off the tin roof.

The few who had gone outside rushed back into the chapel. Women started screaming, and the congregation milled about in a rising panic, knowing that there was trouble but not what it was, as the thuds continued. The next few minutes are confused in my memory, because things happened quickly. I did settle the people down and ordered them to stay inside. Then I got two of our huskiest and most dependable men to go with me to see what the trouble was before anyone got hurt.

A peep out of the door revealed Titus about seventy feet away with a rock in either hand. As soon as he saw us at the door, he let fly with both of them. Fortunately, he was so angry and drunk that his aim was poor. He not only missed us but the whole building. He seemed willing to take on anybody and everybody. Sizing up the situation, the three of us decided to bait him into throwing the two new rocks he had just picked up and rush him from different angles.

We opened the door again and here came the rocks, wide of the mark. Then we put on the rush. When Titus saw us coming, he backed up a few steps and snatched for more ammunition. In doing so, his feet slipped on some loose stones. He fell on his back and rolled over. By then we were on top of him. I never would have believed that three men would have so much trouble subduing one drunk. Titus fought like a wildcat with fists, teeth and finger nails. We got him under control only when one of the men tore his suspenders loose, got a strap around Titus' neck, and choked him.

While Titus lay quiet and tried to get his breath, we took counsel to decide what to do next. In the young man's mood and condition, it seemed too dangerous to turn him loose with so many women and children around who had yet to go home. Some had long distances to travel. There was no telling what Titus would do, especially as he had recovered enough to renew the fight. All we could think of was to put him into my car, drive him to the courthouse, and have him put in jail. No matter what, I would be compelled to bring him before the magistrates anyway.

Now that Titus was well in hand, I first told the congregation that it was safe to go home but to get going as quickly as they could. They needed no urging. Then I got my car and drove it around to the front and we put Titus into the back but not without another battle, which made it necessary for my assistants to sit on him while I drove. The ride down the mountain was a little too exciting, as Titus struggled all the way. Now and then he would get a leg free and try to kick me in the head. I had to lean so far forward that steering became difficult at times.

It was with a sigh of relief that we finally pulled into the village, only to remember that it was Sunday afternoon and that the sheriff would likely be away. If so, we would really have a problem. Happily, when we got to the jail, we found there the Federal officer, who was attending to some chore of his own. Hearing the shouting and cursing from my car, he came over immediately. When I explained the difficulty, he took charge and soon had Titus in a cell, where he could yell and scream to his heart's content. Coming out again, the officer commented, "You all sure took a chance bringing that drunk devil in here. He's a mean one, and people are scared of him. One of these days, somebody's going to fix him!"

After we rested from the ordeal and had gotten something to eat, it was high time to get my valued assistants back up the mountain as it was getting dark and their families were probably getting worried about them by this time. On the way, we stopped off at the magistrate's home to swear out a warrant and to request that a hearing be held as soon as possible. Swift handling of such cases usually had a good effect. He set the time for 10 a.m. the following Thursday, as he was sure that he could get the other two magistrates to sit with him.

When I got my friends home, I asked both of them to send word to Titus' parents that he was in jail and to let them know the time of the hearing. In this case, two messengers were better than one for it was not easy to get messages delivered promptly, and it was important that Titus' father and mother know promptly the state of affairs so that they could visit him and arrange for his defense. It was not really my responsibility but it was good policy to show some good will in the matter. Then with a reasonably good conscience, I returned to home and family, hoping for the best.

The next morning, Titus' mother called me from the mission house, which had the only telephone on the mountain. It was a good three mile walk from her home, which should give her plenty of time to prepare a good tongue lashing if she were so inclined and which I fully expected, for Titus was her only son and badly spoiled. To my relief, the conversation was most friendly. She was sorry that her boy had behaved so badly. I had done exactly right. Her husband was "all broke up" about it but neither of them would be coming down. A few days in jail might be good for Titus, and it was up to him to get out of the mess as best he could.

Her closing words were, "Be as easy on him as you can, but don't let him out of jail until he tells you whar he got his likker." This attitude was not as strange as it might seem. Apparently, it was expected that high spirited youngsters would run afoul of the law sooner or later, and the reaction of the families at times was resigned and even casual. A mountain woman, for example, told me on such an occasion, "You know, it ain't so awful bad for a boy to be sent off to the penitentiary. They l'arn him how to do so many things down thar, how to make furniture, how to bottom chairs, how to carpenter and the like. It's real nice for him."

I allowed another day for Titus to sober up and then went to visit him in jail and to deliver his mother's message. He was subdued but not chastened, suffering more from the aftermath of the binge than from any pangs of conscience. The question about where he got his whiskey was met by stony silence, as might be expected. There was no message for his parents, and they could do as they wished. Yes, he had a lawyer and did not need any help. The visit terminated at this point, since he did not encourage further conversation.

The magistrates' court was duly convened on Thursday at the appointed time, and the trial was brief. It was sad to see that no one from Titus' family came down to be with him, and he did not appear to be on good terms with his lawyer, who was unsteady on his feet. It was obvious that he had prepared for the case in more ways than one. The charge was read, and the presiding magistrate asked the defendant, "How do you plead? Guilty or not guilty?" Titus answered only, "I done it". The response was not conventional, but the magistrates decided not to press the matter and accepted it as a plea of "Guilty!"

It did not take long for me and my witnesses to present our evidence, and cross examination was perfunctory. Then the presiding magistrate addressed Titus, "Do you want to say anything in your defense?" He replied, "No sir, I done it. That's all."

At this point his lawyer got to his feet and began an impassioned speech to the effect that this poor boy had been dreadfully wronged and put upon by supposedly Christian people, when all he was doing was coming to church on Sunday last to worship God, as was his right. What proof was there that there was whiskey in that bottle anyway? Was any test made for drunkenness? As for the fight, didn't the young man have a right to defend himself, when he was attacked by three men and dragged off to jail? Even a dog is allowed to take up for himself. The real charge, in spite of the ignorant defendant's plea, should be placed against the minister who was responsible for a serious crime, the crime of kidnapping, against the peace and dignity of the Commonwealth.

At this time, Titus laughed and even the magistrates had trouble maintaining their dignity. There being nothing further to be said, the magistrates declared a brief recess and requested me to join them in the jury room in fifteen minutes, which I did,

When I met with them, the presiding magistrate said, "We have been talking the case over and have decided to find the defendant guilty in accordance with his plea and the evidence presented. Now all we have to do is to decide on the punishment. We would like to have your advice. We could make it mighty hard for him, but you might not want it that way."

Since this was the fifth time that this situation had arisen for me, I had some definite ideas on what should be done. First of all, I did not want to see a nineteen year old boy sent to the chain gang, as happened so often in those days. Also, I knew that mountain people had little cash money. If Titus were compelled to go to work to earn enough money to pay off a stiff fine, he would doubtless come to the conclusion that there were less expensive ways of showing how big a man he was. Further, since he was noted for his lack of self-control, some threat of jail should hang over his head for a period of time. I made suggestions along these lines and was pleased when they were accepted. Returning to the courtroom, the magistrates fined Titus seventy-five dollars and costs and placed him under peace bond for a year.

After the subsequent formalities had been taken care of, Titus was told that he could go home. On the way out of the courthouse, his lawyer caught up with him and offered to appeal the case, but Titus shrugged him off, saying "Leave me alone. I done paid you your money", and then went outdoors.

He had a long way to go home, almost too far to walk and with too much opportunity to get into trouble in his state of mind. Feeling sorry for him, I wanted to make some gesture of reconciliation. So I stopped him and offered to drive him to the foot of the mountain from where he could easily walk home before dark. Titus did not reply at once. The sheriff was standing nearby. He glanced at me, frowned, and shook his head disapprovingly. I knew that I was taking a chance but thought it well to take the risk. There might be some possibility of making a friend of him, and, if all went well, it would also make a good impression on the mountain people.

Presently, Titus nodded and said "Let's go!" I led him to my car. We got in and drove off. The trip was uneventful, and conversation was nil. Reaching the mountain road turn-off, Titus got out, closed the door, and with a brief "Much obliged!" walked up the grade and out of sight around the curve without glancing back.

As it turned out, we were both satisfied, each in his own way. With his peers, Titus saved face—or thought he did—by proclaiming, "I had that preacher whar I could have got even. Nobody was around and I could have beat him up good. But I let him go." For my part, I had no more trouble with him, nor with any of the other young bucks. It was commonly said afterward around the area, "You better not make no trouble around that man's churches. If you do, he will make you pay or have you sent away sho! That was something of an exaggeration but there was no point in refuting it.

Chapter 17

ROADSIDE CHAT

Nimrod Roach, riding home up the mountain with modest supplies purchased at the courthouse, spied with interest a group of about twenty men up ahead rocking the road. "Rocking the road" was an activity common and necessary in the back sections of the Blue Ridge Mountains. The roads seemed to belong only to those who used them. Both State and County ignored them as much as possible. Votes were few in the hills, and it was easier to forget the roads than to keep them fit for travel, because the wrath of the people would carry little weight at the polls. So if these miserable routes were to be kept open, the local men would have to do it with such tools as they had. Even if road machinery had been available, it would not have had room in which to work since split rail fences and trees bordered closely on the narrow right-of-way.

Most of the roads were one lane affairs, and at intervals there were turnouts where vehicles could pass. There was a certain etiquette controlling the traffic flow, if it could be called that. The descending vehicles were accorded the right-of-way because, on the steep mountain grades, the brakes on wagons or autos could not always be trusted and then too backing downhill was safer and easier than trying it uphill. The procedure was this: on approaching a turnout, the driver of a wagon or buggy would shout a few times. If there was no answer, he would drive on and repeat the performance at the next one. If there was an answer, the ascending vehicle would be driven into the by-pass, and the driver would wait until the way was clear. In the case of an automobile, blasts from the horn would take the place of the shouts. Usually there was so little traffic that these encounters would often result in a roadside chat and an exchange of news and gossip.

At best, winding, narrow mountain roads were very rough and no place for joy rides. Driving required close and careful attention to prevent mishaps and worse. The deep, red ruts were bad enough, but the cross drains could be dangerous. There were no culverts and, to take off the up-slope water, shallow ditches were dug across the road and mounded up on the low side. These were excellent places to break an axle where one was driving a car or a wagon. It might seem a waste of time and labor to do much work on such thoroughfares, which were little more than wagon trails, but without even minimum attention, they would disintegrate and the people would be virtually cut off from the outside world. The roads simply had to be kept open, and it was almost a matter of life and death.

During the winter months, rocks and even boulders of various sizes on the slopes above the road bed, especially where there were cuts, were often loosened by alternating freezes and thaws and also by the wash of many rains. Numbers of them would roll down onto the road and become a nuisance to traffic, such as it was, as well as clogging the drains alongside. Mountain people are difficult to enlist in common efforts, so highly independent and individualistic are they. But when their lifeline was threatened, they turned out in force to cut away fallen trees, remove dangerous stones, and to dig out and clean the ditches. Spring time was rocking time, though in emergencies volunteers would be summoned at any time. This operation was not only a physical requirement but was also a social function, since the men enjoyed visiting each other away from the women folks. The main difficulty was keeping them on the job as the work moved along, because labor tended to be diluted with too much gossip and horseplay.

In a few moments, Nimrod encountered the vanguard of the task force and shouted greetings:

"Hi, Matt!"

"Hi, Luke! Hope you're sober!"

"How's your pa now, Tiny? That's good."

"Say, Squitch! Who's in charge of this here job?..."

"Rius is? ... Whar's he at? ... Up ahead? Bye, for now"

Making his way through the toilers and around the bend, he spotted Rius Shoales, sitting on a boulder in the shade of a giant oak tree growing beside the way. He was smoking a pipe and going through the motions of bossing the job but not exhausting himself. Rius' name is worth a moment's notice as it was a contraction of Honorius Addie Alexander and Silas Shoales. No one knew the origin of Honorius, but Addie was his aunt and Alexander and Silas his two uncles. This was evidently an attempt to keep the peace between jealous relatives. The family name Shoales must have been Schultz originally, derived perhaps from a Hessian prisoner settled in the Valley of Virginia at the time of the American Revolution.

Being in no hurry, Nimrod reined up his horse, dismounted, and tethered the animal to a nearby fence rail where it was cool. Then he sat beside Rius, who moved over to make room for him.

"Ain't seen you for some time. How's your family?" asked Nimrod.

"They's all tol'able peart, Nimrod. How's Quillie and your young uns?"

"Well as common, Rius, thanks you. Well as common. Why ain't you working out there with Luke and Bunce and Gossie and the rest of the boys, if you don't take no harm in my asking. It's as much your road as theirs."

"I got this misery in my back. It ketches me every time I stoop over. So, I'm a setting here to see the job git done. If somebody wasn't watching, some of 'em would frolic around and maybe sneak down into the bushes to git out of doing their share. Anyways, I suspicions that thar's a jug of likker hid somewhars, and somebody will be gitting powerful thirsty for a nip soon. Got to watch 'em! Got to watch 'em!"

"Well, you was always a good hand for watching other folks work, Rius. I didn't see you at Bogey's funeral last week. How come?"

"This here misery was gitting bad on me then, Nimrod. It's a right fur piece to Bogey's place for a fact and I jest couldn't git up 'ar. Big crowd?"

"Sizeable, sizeable. They had a preacher to come up from Shenandoah to preach the funeral. He done right good, but he didn't preach Bogey neither to heaven nor to hell; didn't know Bogey too well, I guess. I hated to see Bogey go. He was so common and done me many a good turn."

"Did the family take it hard?"

"Not too hard, Rius, Bogey being so bad off so long. The women made right smart noise, but only his old woman fell out."

"Sho wish I could have been thar. Was you down to the courthouse today for something special?"

"No, jest to pay some taxes and git some fixings for my wife. My cabbage's heading up good, and Quillie wants to be ready to make plenty of sauerkraut. We run out too soon this year, and I sure miss it bad."

"Needn't have, Nimrod; needn't have. Why don't you buy canned sauerkraut down at Perkin's store to tide you over?"

"No sir, not me. That slopped-up, store-boughten sauerkraut ain't worth a damn! I wouldn't feed it to a hog, much less my family".

"Maybe 'twarn't made at the cannery at the right time. It's got to be harvested and hauled to the cannery on the full moon or it won't be fit to eat."

"You might be right, Rius. They say you got to be careful 'bout the right time for things. Last year, I planted 'taters in the sign of the goat. They come strong and didn't taste good. Will Gerald set out his sweet 'taters in the sign of the crawfish, and they turned out tough and stringy."

"Sho is hard to keep up with these here signs, Nimrod. Seems to me the best time to do your work is when you kin. Waiting for signs throws you back, 'specially if the weather gits bad. Did you hear how Tim Barker's trial is coming out while you was at the courthouse? Starting yesterday, it should be finished today."

"I don't rightly know, Rius. I went and listened for a spell this morning but didn't have time to stay long. Folks say chances are he'll be sent away. He did hurt Fuzzy Allen right bad with a rock, you know. What's against him is that he run and dodged. But the worst sign I saw when I was thar, John Hammond, Tim's lawyer, was talking to the jury and was reading the Bible to 'em. Now John never reads the Bible to a jury 'less he knows he's got a powerful weak case."

"Too bad. It's going to be mighty hard on Tim's family. His pa depends on Tim to help him on the farm. Young folks sho seem to git into a pack of trouble these days. They won't listen to the old folks at all; jest plain hard-headed, Nimrod. That's what they are. Thar's my gal, Katy. Henry Geer's been looking at her for some time now but she don't favor him none. Henry's a good steady boy and a hard worker. We tell her he'd make a good husband and if she don't look out she'll be a old maid, but she don't pay us no mind. She tosses her head and says she ain't ready to fetch and carry for no man, no ways!"

"I agrees with you, Rius, I don't know what they're coming to. I grieves 'bout it a lot. T'other day, I kotched my boy, Sam, chunking rocks at Pap Gray's hogs while they was out in the woods hunting acorns. He's still kind of young, but he knows better. I breshed him a little and hope he'll behave, but you know how 'tis with the younguns."

"Gitting on to something else, I hear you 'most lost your calf t'other day, Nimrod."

"Come close to it. The critter got hold of a green apple and tried to swallow it whole and nigh choked to death. I wasn't home but Quillie was thar and heard the calf making an awful noise. She grabbed the broom, and, while one of my boys held the calf steady, she rammed the handle down its gullet and fixed whatever it was. It's a fine calf. I'd of hated to lose it."

"You was mighty lucky. I don't know nothing 'bout doctoring animals but I'd of thought the broom handle might have made it worse or punched a hole somewhars. But Quillie cured it, so it ain't up to me to say aught."

"We was lucky all right. Now, tell me something, Rius; as I was riding along South River toward the mountains, I seen old man Mose Shifflett out in the fields acting funny. Is he all right?"

"How you mean acting funny?"

"Hard to explain. He'd walk this way a little, shade his eyes, and look up at the sky. Then he'd circle around some and do the same thing again. Now and then, he'd hold his arm out and sight along it. Once I seen him squat down and squint over the top of a fence post. He was mighty took up with his queer doings. I hollered at him but he never did pay me no mind, jest kept squinting. Looked funny to me."

"Nothing was wrong with old man Mose," said Rius laughing. "His mouth was watering for some new honey, that's all. He was studying the beelines."

"Studying beelines? What for?"

"To find bee trees. Long's you lived in the mountains, you ought to know something 'bout that, Nimrod."

"I don't want nothing to do with bees. Once, when I was a boy, I messed around my uncle's bee gums, and the bees come at me like a cloud and stung the blazes out of me. I don't want nothing to do with 'em. How does all that walking in circles and squinting here and thar help find a bee tree?"

"It's this way, Nimrod. You see, the honey flow is on right now and the bees are working lots of flowers, 'specially clover and locusts. They're loading it up fast and hauling it home to cure. Some bees has homes in bee trees and some in gums. When they're headed home with a heavy load, they fly low and kind of slow. These are the ones old Mose is watching, 'specially those flying towards the woods 'cause thar's whar the bee trees are."

"Thar's lots of trees in the woods. How can Mose spot the right ones?"

"Tain't easy but old man Mose is kind of sharp at it. He's been doing it a long time. He studies the beelines, sighting from this here place and that thar place, maybe lots of places. When some of the lines look like they might cross out in the woods somewhars, he takes a bearing and walks towards the spot. When he gits thar, he walks 'round and 'round real slow looking up in the trees and listening for the buzzing of the bees. He don't miss many times, 'deed he don't."

"What does he do when he finds it? 'Specially when the bees is up real high?"

"It's this way, Nimrod. He makes a bargain with the man what owns the tree to share the honey. Then he gits together a bunch of the men what likes wild honey and enjoys a little lark at night. Old Mose generally brings along some moonshine and this helps too. He never invites the sheriff nor none of his deputies, you can bet. They all goes out with axes, butcher knives, a bucket or two, and lanterns to see by. When they git to the tree, they whirl in and cut it down, split it open, and dig out the honey."

"What I don't understand, Rius, is how they keep from gitting all stung up. Do they make a fire and smoke the bees?"

"No sir. That wouldn't help much, and besides fire might git away in the woods and make bad trouble. Oh, some will git stung, all right, but not much. You see, all that pounding on the tree with the axes in the dark, where the bees can't see, confuses 'em, and all they do is crawl 'round, not knowing what to do. It's a good thing to wear thick clothes and be sure to tie your britches legs tight and as low down as you kin. If you don't, some bees sure will crawl up in your britches and make you dance later on."

"They ain't going to crawl up mine. I ain't going nigh them. I had my dose once. I don't think a gallon or two of honey's worth all that trouble, no ways."

"Why not, Nimrod? Wild honey's the best kind of honey. It's real sweet, and it's got a strong taste."

"My uncle says different, Rius. He keeps bees like I told you but he changed from gums to these here patent hives. He won't eat honey from narwhars else. He says wild honey ain't fit to eat."

"That's a curious way to talk. What's the matter with wild honey?"

"Everything's wrong with it, he says."

"Such as?"

"First thing, it's dirty. My uncle says thar's no way to dig out that honey without gitting trash and dirt all in it. Next thing, the old comb gits dug out with the new comb and it's brown and tough and bitter—no wonder wild honey tastes strong. But the worst thing is what you see in the honey once it's in the buckets—bits of bees—wings—legs—and stings that git stuck in your mouth and tongue and give a body a fit. You'll find grub bees, the baby bees, that look like worms, all mixed in it too. It's enough to turn your stomach, Rius."

"Now look here, Nimrod, you don't have to eat a mess like that if you know what to do. All you got to do is put it on the stove and heat it careful like, just enough to melt the wax so's you kin strain it through a cloth to take out the trash and stuff. When it cools, you kin lift the wax off the top in a cake and thar's the honey ready for your biscuits as nice as you please! What's wrong with that?"

"I wouldn't be able to fergit how nasty it was…. Looks like the boys is gitting ready to quit for the day…. Hey, it's late… Plague take it! The time clean got away from me! I'd better make a beeline for home, if I know what's good for me. Bye, Rius. You come visit."

"You come too, Nimrod."

"Sho will, if I live."

"See you soon."

"So do! So do!"

Chapter 18

MINDING THE STORE

Perkins General Store stood where the mountain road forked off from the low road which led ultimately to Hood and beyond. The name was grander than the building, an unpainted frame structure that had grown grey with age. The windows, coated with grime, had not been washed for years. The sign above the entrance was askew and the paint was peeling off, rendering it almost unreadable. The porch roof sagged at one end where the base of the front post had rotted away due to a big leak in the down spout of the guttering. The proprietor answered all unfavorable comment on this long standing condition by promising, "I'll get it fixed up soon's my work lets up some."

The front steps were wobbly and had to be mounted with care. For the convenience of the public, there were, on each side of the front door, pews discarded by some church which judged them too rickety for safety. Each was decorated by scores of initials carved in the woodwork of the backrest and seat so that there was scarcely a smooth place left. From within the store, there drifted through the door an indefinable odor that seemed to be a mixture of coal oil, molasses, and rancid salt pork. It was a carbon copy of hundreds of country stores in the rural South.

On this hot July morning, Tump Perkins, owner and postmaster, sat in one of the pews with his stout, jolly wife, Portia, waiting for whatever patronage that might come their way, and trying to get some meager relief from the heat with palm leaf fans. Helping them wait were:

Lively Gerald, a callow youth of nineteen, who craved recognition as an adult and was prone to butt into grown-up conversation. His elders accepted him with amused tolerance.

Asa Carter, a veteran hypochondriac of uncertain age, who was supported by a school teacher wife.

Matt Powell, a brawny middle-aged lumberman, who had seen better days, and was above the local average in education.

There was little traffic along the dusty roads. The nearby mountains seemed to quiver in the heat. The air was still with a faint touch of a breeze now and then. There was a heavy quiet, broken at times by the whirring of cicadas and the complaint of mourning doves in the nearby woods.

A listlessness had settled over the group, and Tump Perkins was dozing. Presently, Matt Powell yawned, mopped his face and neck with a dingy handkerchief, and addressed the storekeeper:

"Wake up there, Tump. You got anything cold to drink back there in the store?"

Tump came to with a start and objected, "I wasn't asleep. I was jest thinking. No. I ain't got nothing cold to drink. Man didn't bring ice this morning. Maybe it all melted before he could git this far. All I got is some cokes setting in warm water waiting for the ice. Business is so bad that if I could sell you a drink, I'd figure I had a big day."

"Maybe I'll go to the well in a little while," mumbled Matt, yawning again. "I surely would like an ice cold drink right now."

"You hadn't ought to drink anything ice cold right now in this weather. Chances are that it would make your belly all swole up, 'specially if you're all het up!", warned Asa Carter.

"I'd chance it," replied Matt. "Couldn't be worse than dying with the heat."

"Hey" exclaimed Lively Gerald. "Thar's a cloud of dust up the road. Somebody's coming this-a-way."

All fell silent and watched the approaching dust cloud for a few moments.

"Looks like a fellow driving a wagon and two horses", opined Matt, squinting. "Hard to tell from here."

"Wonder who'd be coming down from the mountains on a day like this?" asked Lively of no one in particular.

"I tell you what, Lively", answered Portia. "He's driving so slow, why don't you run up the road and see who 'tis and then run back and tell us? You're young and peart."

"Don't tease the boy", chided Tump. "Portia, you're jest as curious as he is with so little happening today."

"I bet you that's Joe William's team for sure", said Lively peering into the distance. "Look at that white horse!"

"Look again, boy", scoffed Matt. "Those are mules, one white and one brown."

"You all wait a bit and you'll see who 'tis", suggested Portia. "Anybody's think we was expecting an angel of the Lord!"

The wait required not more than ten minutes until the dusty team and driver pulled up in front of the store.

"I think it's nobody but Nicey Shifflett", offered Matt Powell. "I won't know for sure until he gets all that dirt washed off his face."

"Hi there, Nicey !", greeted Tump, getting up and walking to the edge of the porch. "How are you? How's your old woman and young 'uns?"

"We all as well as common", responded Nicey, taking off his hat and fanning with it. "Whew! Mighty hot ain't it? What you all doing sitting 'round and loafing like tomorrow ain't never coming."

"I'm jest looking after these lazy folks", laughed Portia. "I have a hard time keeping 'em out of trouble and from lying bout their neighbors."

"Truth is, Nicey", put in Tump, "Portia here is hoping you got some news to tell us. Drive your team 'round to the side of the store whar it's shady. Water the critters if they need it. Then come and set a spell."

Nicey got down and led the team to the place designated. After he was out of sight, Lively ventured the comment, "Nicey's looking right good, ain't he?"

"Naw. He looks kind of peaked to me," said Asa Carter. "He needs some proper vittles. I bet his old woman don't feed him nothing but fried stuff. That tears a man's stomach to pieces."

"Asa, you got such a mixed up head you think everybody's sick like you like to think you are", rebuked Portia. "Here's Nicey's back and it's 'bout time. You better take up for yourself, Nicey. Asa thinks you look thin and dragged down."

"I'm always thin in summer. Heat and hard work does it, but Asa wouldn't understand that, would you, Asa?" asked Nicey accusingly.

"Everybody picks on me like I never hit a honest day's work in my life", whined Asa. "Why, Nicey, when I was your age I could out work any two of you without sweating. But one hot day like this the monkey got me and I ain't been right since."

"If that's your excuse, Asa, you better stick to it", grunted Tump. "People will believe that as quick as any other tale. Nicey, are you going to some wedding or a wake? I see you got your Sunday shirt and Sunday overhauls on, and today is only Thursday. How come?"

"These is now my work clothes", explained Nicey. "They used to be my Sunday clothes, but my old lady told me I was 'bliged to git some new ones. She said she was 'shamed to go with me to church on Sundays 'cause I looked so sorry."

"Now, that hurts me real bad, as good a friend as I been to you", groaned Tump. "You went and bought new clothes and you didn't buy 'em from me; and I thought you was the one person I could count on."

"Before you git to hurting too bad to wait on me, I got to take home a sack of meal, five pounds of coffee, five pounds of fatback, a sack of sugar, and a Harris hoe. Think you can scrape that together for me?" asked Nicey, quite unmoved by Tump's complaint.

"Now, don't get all fired up, Nicey", replied Tump appeasingly. "How 'bout letting me sell you some good pipe tobacco so you can smoke while we set here and visit? I got in some yesterday real fresh."

"Nope. I raise and cure my own tobacco on my place. It's a man's tobacco, good and strong, not like that sissy store bought stuff which ain't even fit for a woman to smoke. If you don't mind, I'll light up my pipe now—meaning no harm of course."

"Help yourself", responded Tump coolly. "Look here, I noticed that you got four big barrels on your wagon. What are you going to do with 'em, Nicey? They ain't mash barrels now, is they?"

"Course not, Tump, you know they ain't. I don't make no likker. I don't like jail that good. I borrowed 'em to haul water from the creek. It's still running, I hope, because my spring's gone dry."

"Yep, it is. Water's powerful low though."

"When you git home with that water, Nicey, you better bile it", warned Asa. "When a creek's been low that long, the water's full of fever. I drunk low creek water once and got real sick. Ain't been right since."

"Oh, I don't aim to drink it. Walter Simmons lets me and my family git drinking water from his spring. It's done got weak, so he's 'bliged to be sort of careful. That's why I'm starting to haul water for the mules and for washing 'til my spring comes back."

"Most springs is still running 'round here. Did you do anything to your spring, Nicey?" inquired Lively Gerald.

"Nothing much. I cleaned it out last April and reset some of the stones."

"Thar now", continued Lively. "Did you happen to kill a spring-keeper while you was doing it?

"Maybe. But what's that got to do with it?"

"Like what the old folks say, 'Kill a spring-keeper and your spring will run dry.' Jest like everybody knows if you kill a frog, your cow will go dry."

"I never heard such foolishness in my life", said Nicey crossly. "It ain't rained in weeks. When it's dry, springs go dry. That's all. If it wasn't for this shade and that hot sun, I wouldn't set here and listen to such fool talk. Beats me what some ignorant people will believe!"

"You mark my words, Nicey," broke in Asa again. "Don't use that water 'less you bile it. It's plain pizen. It kin kill folks."

"Go on, Asa!" laughed Portia. "You love to talk 'bout sickness and death more 'n anybody I ever say. I bet you'd feel bad if you ever caught yourself feeling good."

"Thar you go, making fun of an old man and his miseries jest 'cause you're fat and sassy! The Lord might punish you for saying that. He might take you away when you ain't looking for it!" complained Asa.

"Maybe! Maybe! But I ain't going to order my coffin on your say-so!" retorted Portia.

"Asa, you're always looking at the worst side of everything", accused Matt Powell. "You're bilious just like my preacher. He's down on everything but money. Why don't you take some soda?"

"Too hard on the stomach."

"Take some aspirin then", prescribed Matt.

"Too hard on the heart".

"I give up", said Matt, throwing up his hands. "I never saw a man work so hard at being sick just to keep from working."

"Quit plaguing poor old Asa", commanded Tump with mock sympathy. "Why ain't you working at your sawmill today anyway, Matt? Did your help finally starve to death on the poor pay you give 'em?"

"Didn't dare to fire up the boiler. Woods are so dry that one good spark would make them explode like they were soaked with kerosene, so I'm just killing time. Say, Tump, I'm hungry. Get me some crackers, a box of sardines, and a piece of your rat cheese."

"Give me fifty cents and git 'em yourself. It's too hot to wait on customers 'less they're buying enough to make it worthwhile. Don't slice that cheese too thick now!"

"I'm not going to slice it too thin either. I'll need some water to wash it down. Are you going to charge me for that?"

"Not if you're going to the well and git it for yourself", growled Tump. "Quit fussing. Storekeepers got to make a little money jest like you thieving lumbermen. If this drought keeps up, I'll be lucky to stay in business. You complainers give me a headache."

Matt laughed, got up, and handed Tump a fifty cent piece. Then he went into the store to fill his order. In a few moments he returned, sat down on the steps and started opening the can of sardines while the others watched the operation silently. Presently, Lively felt moved to renew the conversation.

"Say, Tump, you was talking 'bout having a headache. Do you know the best way to cure a headache?"

"Thar ain't no best way."

"O yes, they is. My grandma says you go wash your head in a spring jest before the sun comes up and you're cured quick."

"Well jest suppose you try it the next time you git a headache, which ain't going to be long from now if you keep on talking 'bout your fool notions", threatened Tump. "Anyways, I wouldn't want to wake up them pore little spring-keepers you been talking 'bout."

"Don't mind him, Lively", said Portia soothingly. "By the way, you been here at the store most of the morning—not that you ain't welcome—but ain't you got some work these days?"

"No'm. I been helping pa but it's so dry thar ain't no plowing nor weeding. The fences is all fixed and the fence rows is cleaned out. I been looking for some odd jobs all the way to the courthouse but thar ain't nothing nowhars."

"Maybe you ought to leave the mountains and look for work way away somewhere", mumbled Matt biting into the slice of cheese.

"That's what they tells me. Sho ain't nothing much 'round here for young folks 'cept farming, and thar ain't no farms for sale even if you got the money. Then too, I jest don't know how I'd make out away from the hills. I ain't knowed nothing else, and I ain't got no education neither."

"Well, if you ain't going away, you better marry and settle down before you git into trouble like some of the other boys", counseled Tump.

"I ain't figuring on that. I ain't ready to settle down," replied Lively emphatically.

"You got a girl, Lively?" asked Nicey, with a wink at the others.

"Naw. What makes you ask that?"

"I seen you last Sunday helping that yellow haired girl over the fence. You two were giggling and hollering a lot. I jest bet you were tickling her or something. She didn't look like she hated you none. How 'bout it?"

"Lively! Look at you! You're turning all red. Is it so? You got a girl?" exclaimed Portia.

"No'm. She was no special girl. We was jest having a nice time. I ain't got no money to think 'bout gitting married. You can't live off these rocks. They ain't 'taters, and they ain't meat!"

"He's right", sighed Matt. "I married my wife when I had no work. We made out but we saw a mighty hard time. Unless something opens up in these parts, the young folks will just have to go away. There is nothing for them here except hard times."

"You're right!" agreed Asa. "It's a hard, hard life for young and old. You're born, you grow up, you work hard, you git old, you die, and what does it all amount to?"

"Asa, I never heard such sorry talk in my life" objected Tump, scandalized. "You spread more misery than any man I know. Don't you ever think happy? Don't you ever look forwards to something good?"

"Nothing 'cept to leave this earth. I know I ain't for long. I don't know why the good Lord don't take me away", replied Asa mournfully.

"Cheer up, Asa. You are going to die all right. You are going to die as sure as hell if you just live long enough."

"Come on, Tump," said Nicey getting to his feet. "'Git me my things and let me git away from here while I got some strength left. Asa's got me so low in my mind I can hardly budge. I got to git going anyway."

"I shore don't fault you none", sympathized Tump. "Come on in the store and pick out what you want. I jest might find a little nip of something somewhars to perk you up some."

"Well, I guess that 'bout ties up the sack for now," sighed Portia. "I 'spect it's 'bout time for me to git home and see if the bread's riz and to look the salad greens. So long boys. Take care. Be seeing you soon—if I live."

Chapter 19

FEED STORE THEOLOGY

Noah Collins, proprietor of the Blue Ridge Feed Store and church elder, was in a grumpy mood. The untimely arrival of customers had interrupted his afternoon siesta, which he usually spent pillowed among the sacks of grain stored in a side room at the back of the store. Then too, he found that Benny Snow, his eighteen year old summer helper, was taking his time moving the fifty sacks of laying mash off the loading platform into the shed, especially since it looked like a storm was working up. The weather was hot and close for June, not a breeze stirring, and this did not improve his disposition as he stood behind the counter scowling at the page in the ledger bearing the charge account of Lay Fat Lewis, who was standing before him.

Lay Fat Lewis, whose given name was a corruption of the illustrious name of our great French hero, Lafayette, was having a difficult time trying to make a living on his poor mountain farm for his wife and for his four children, Tim Fat, Lady Fat, Sissie Fat, and Joe Fat. He needed several sacks of fertilizer to perk up his worn out soil, but this required an extension of his shaky credit with the store and the owner was not pleased at the prospect.

"Look here, Lay Fat", grumbled Noah, "you're way behind in paying what you owe. I got to pay my bills too, you know. I'd like to help you, but you got to do some ketching up before you git too deep in the hole and pull me in with you."

Lay Fat turned red with embarrassment and looked away for a moment and then faced his creditor. "I don't fault you none in worrying 'bout it. You been mighty patient with me. I look to git a fa'r price for my cabbage crop. Then too, the Park people been after me to sell 'em my farm. I jest might do it. My land is real sorry. Looks to me I could do better to leave these parts and git a new start somewhars else. But I got to keep a-going this season. I don't aim to beat you out of nothing, Noah. You been good to me. You kin count on me soon's I git hold of some money. Times have been hard."

"I know you mean all right, Lay Fat," replied Noah, softening a little. "Do the best you can soon's you can. I can't carry too much on my books and stay in business. You in a hurry? ... You ain't? Well let me wait on Hezekiah Shifflett here first and Will Holmes next, and then I'll git your fertilizer. What can 1 do for you, Hezzy?"

"I want about twenty pounds of white corn seed."

"I thought you had done putting in your crop."

"I did and my corn come up good, but the crows, and the cut worms, and the cold spring mighty nigh ruint me. I got to plant some all over again."

"That don't seem right, Hezzy. You're a good Christian man and a deacon in your church. How come you didn't come off better'n that?"

"I guess it's like the Good Book says 'bout the just and the unjust."

"Which are you, Hezzy?" asked Will Holmes, breaking into the conversation with a wink at Noah Collins.

"I ain't saying. The Lord decides that. I figure that we all has equal chances down here. I ain't complaining. I'll make out."

"Here's your corn, and good luck, Hezzy", said Noah, handing him a heavy sack. "Thanks for the prompt pay, meaning no harm of course. All right, Will, what can I do for you?"

"Nothing, Noah. It looks like it's going to be a terrible storm coming down from Swift Run. I thought I'd step in here for a spell and see what happens, if you don't mind. I'd hate to be ketched out on the road."

"I thought it was gitting powerful dark", observed Noah, looking out one of the dingy windows. "The wind's coming up strong too. Hey, Benny, you got them sacks of laying mash under cover yet?"

"Most done, Mr. Noah. They ain't going to git wet", answered Benny Snow from the rear of the store.

"They better not. You can come up front 'til the storm blows out,.. Man! That was a close lightning hit!" exclaimed Noah, startled by a sharp crack of lightning, followed in an instant by a crash of thunder. "Lay Fat, you and Hezzy had better see 'bout your teams. Take 'em 'round to the south side of the store. They'll be better off thar. . .Oh, That's whar they are?. . Good."

"Man, oh, man! It's really starting to come down now," he observed, looking out the window again.

Just then, the front door burst open, and a drenched figure stumbled in, pausing only to shoulder the door shut against the blowing sheets of rain.

"Hey! Who we got here?" queried Will. "Looks like some big fish done jumped clear out the creek, Oh! Tain't no fish. It's jest Casty Groves. Wring yourself out, Casty, and enjoy some good company for a change."

"Hi, there Casty. Don't pay no attention to Will. You shore are wet. Maybe we can find a clothesline 'round here somewhars so we can pin you up to dry out", welcomed Noah.

Casty, whose name was really Cassidy, ignored the gibes while he tried to see what he could do about his clothing, which was little except to remove his coat, wring it out and hang it on a peg to dry. The others watched him and offered teasing suggestions until he finally gave up and sat down on a convenient nail keg. Then, he faced his companions, smiled broadly, and commented, "Don't you all bother 'bout me none. I'm fine, praise God! That thar rain's a sod-buster now. It's going to break the drought. We shore needed it. Thank the Lord!"

"You seem to be mighty happy, in spite of looking like a drowned cat", said Noah. "They tell me that you got religion at the revival last week."

"You heard right", replied Casty. "I seen the light. I'm on my way to heaven."

"Glad you got right at last. 'Deed I am. You can stand changing your ways. Jest you take care you don't trip up!" advised Noah.

"What do you mean? What makes you think I'm going to trip up?"

"You sound a mite brash", accused Noah. "I've seen lots of people git religion and in six month's time they're back whar they started from.

You was powerful sot in your ways to change all of a sudden. See that you don't git so stuck up that you think you're better'n other folks. The devil'll sneak up on you before you know it. I done seen it many a time."

"You're wrong there", asserted Casty. "I've changed. I'm happy and my wife's happy. I'm a new man!"

"Your wife shore could stand something to make her happy, seeing the hard time you done give her", commented Lay Fat, deciding to take part in the conversation.

"See! See! That proves I done changed!" exclaimed Casty, turning red. "Week before last I'd of knocked your head off for saying that but I forgive you. Why don't you come out to the revival, Lay Fat? It would do you a world of good."

"I don't take no stock in revivals", replied Lay Fat.

"Why not?"

"I been baptized seven times and it ain't took yet."

"How was you baptized?" inquired Hezzy. "It's got to be done right, you know."

Just then there was a sharp crack of lightning and a crash.

"Whoops!" shouted Will Holmes. "By grannies, that lightning bolt was a close one. That noise jest 'bout split my ears. Smell that funny smell. I sure don't want one closer 'n that!"

"Benny, run take a look and see if the horses are all right", ordered Noah. "My notion is that the lightning hit a tree in the woods back of my shed."

"A bolt like that kind of sobers you up, don't it? It's the Lord's way of teaching us manners when we git too perky", pontificated Will.

"The horses are standing steady", reported Benny, returning. "Kind of nervous, but they don't look as scared as you all do."

"Your manners can stand some mending", reproved Noah. "You're as scared as any of us."

"No, I ain't", asserted Benny. "You see, the way I look at it, nothing's going to kill you 'less it's your time to go. My time ain't come yet. It's coming some day, but it ain't today. So I ain't worrying."

"Suit yourself, Benny. I ain't going to argue. I agree you ain't dead yet. Say, whar was we when that lightning struck?"

"Hezzy was asking Lay Fat was he baptized right", Will reminded him. "Lay Fat, how did they baptize you?"

"I don't know what you mean. I was immersed. Wasn't that all right?"

"Was you put under the water forwards or backwards?" asked Hezzy.

"1 don't rightly remember", answered Lay Fat. "What difference does it make? I didn't feel right 'bout it afterwards none of the times."

"Feelings don't matter, so long's it's done right", asserted Hezzy. "It's got to be done in deep running water, immersed all the way three times forwards."

"My preacher says it's three times forwards and three times backwards to be right", put in Casty.

"He might say that," chuckled Will Holmes, "but I was at one of his baptizings one time after a revival. He had a time with one sister. She was big and fat, and jest before she was to go down into the water, she got real happy and was shouting and hollering and jumping up and down by the time he got hold of her. She got out of his grip two or three times and like to have drowned. She was immersed all right, but I bet your preacher don't know if he did it right or not, and, furthermore, I don't believe he's worrying 'bout it none. He shore was glad to get rid of that sister."

"All this talk is plumb foolishness", objected Noah Collins. "How you baptize don't count. It's what you believe in your heart and how much you want to do right. If your heart ain't right, a hundred preachers and a river full of water can't do you no good, even if they baptize you a hundred times."

"I agrees with you," put in Benny. "If you believe, thar's more'n one way to baptize. Look at the Methodists, they sprinkle. Look at the 'Piscopalians, they pour. Both of 'em look like they do all right."

"No, 'tain't all right neither", insisted Hezzy Shifflett vehemently. "It's got to be done right in the right church whar the doctrine's sound and whar the preaching's straight from the Bible. Now you take me. I believe every word in the Bible, jest like it's writ down."

"You do, do you?" inquired Will Holmes. "Then how 'bout the place in the Bible whar it says 'Answer a fool according to his folly', and then whar it says, 'Don't answer a fool according to his folly'?"

"I guess it all depends on what kind of fool you're talking to", suggested Benny.

"Answer me this one", baited Will. "Who killed Goliath?"

"David, of course", answered Hezzy scornfully.

"That's what it says in the Book of Samuel one I. But in the Book of Samuel two I, you find that somebody else done the job. Now what do you make of that?"

"Well, maybe it comes back to the business of answering a fool according to his folly", grumbled Will. "But I plain don't hold with nobody what takes the Bible to disprove the Bible. The main thing is the Book is the best thing we got to go by, even if some smart folks try to mess it up."

"You're right 'bout that," agreed Noah. "The Book says enough things straight enough to keep us busy 'til Judgment Day if we put our minds to it. All this argument between church folks don't make no sense to me, and it ain't fitting nohow."

"Whooey!" exclaimed Benny looking out the window. "Thar's a powerful lot of water out thar. The road looks like a river. Hope it don't wash out before I git home."

"Hush up, Benny", reproved Noah. "Why don't you listen to what we're saying? You jest might learn something. Like I was saying, I don't like to see church folks quarreling with each other. I admits I do some myself but it all makes for too many hard feelings and too many churches, each one claiming it's the only one fit to be called a church."

"Well, folks got to stand up for what they believe", responded Casty Groves.

"That's all right if they know what they're talking 'bout and ain't jest being hardheaded like some folks I know. I've heard lots of preachers of different churches 'round here shout and exhort and thar ain't a dime's worth of difference between 'em when you git down to rock bottom. It's hardheadedness and it ain't truth what stirs up hard feelings."

"Do you believe in preaching the truth?" asked Casty.

"Sure I do", answered Noah. "But what makes you think your church has got it all?"

"We believe what we believe and stick to it!"

"Look out, Noah!" warned Will. "You're gitting all het up. If you two go running down that road, you'll keep on forever. All you need to do is to believe in the Lord and stay with the Bible. We all are heading for the same place and all churches look mighty alike."

"Tain't so", countered Benny. "Thar's a heap of difference between churches."

"Name 'em", challenged Will, jabbing his fore finger at Benny.

"Well, the Baptists won't let nobody come to the Lord's Table 'less he's a Baptist, but the Methodists'll let anybody come. The Holy Rollers don't think anybody's saved less he gits happy and talks with tongues. Dunkards pray from the heart but 'Piscopalians can't pray without reading from a book. Disciples won't take anybody in 'til he's big enough to profess faith, but 'Piscopalians baptize little bitty babies what don't know nothing."

"Those 'Piscopalians do good work but I can't go along with 'em," commented Hezzy.

"Why not?" asked Benny.

"Well, they say in church that they believe in the Cath'lic Church. I can't stand for that. I got no use for Cath'lics. You can't trust 'em."

"I'll lay my bottom dollar you don't know a single Cath'lic in the world. Now, tell us right here what Cath'lics you know. Jest name one. They ain't none in these parts", said Lay Fat defiantly.

"I don't know none", responded Hezzy, "but my preacher knows a heap 'bout 'em. and he tells us what kind of folks they is. He knows all right."

"I hope your preacher knows the Lord better'n he seems to know 'bout Cath'lics", asserted Lay Fat.

"What makes you say that?" asked Hezzy belligerently.

"Well, if a man knows the Lord", replied Lay Fat, "he lives by what he preaches, such as do as you would be done by, paying your just debts, keeping your word, and things like that."

"Now, jest exactly what are you gitting at? What you got against my preacher?" demanded Hezzy.

"Here it is nearly June", said Lay Fat, squinting at the large calendar on the wall behind the counter, which advertised lumber for all purposes. "Yes sir, it's close to June. Last March, your preacher asked me to bring him four cords of fire wood. I took him the wood and he ain't paid me to this day. He ought to pay his debts. I need that money to help me pay what I owe to Noah here."

"If you knowed more, you'd be more just", reproved Hezzy. "Our preacher don't git paid except every quarter. That's the agreement we got with him. The second quarter is nearly up. He'll git his money and you'll git yours—don't worry. Right now the poor man probably ain't got one nickel to rub against another in his pocket. In between times, he sees hard times like you and me."

"I say thar's too many churches and too many preachers for the people", observed Noah. "Here in Greene County, we got six different kinds of churches for little over 3,000 folks, counting even babies. Fewer churches would make fatter preachers. Like it is now, a preacher's got to have a circuit and run himself ragged, or he and his family will starve. Don't make no sense."

"Shore don't make no sense", said Casty emphatically. "Now, if everybody belonged to the right church, we wouldn't be like a bunch of hogs in a thunderstorm, all squealing and running 'round, not knowing which way to go.

"What church is the right one?" asked Benny.

"My church. Else I wouldn't belong to it."

"What makes you say that?" demanded Lay Fat.

"Because it's got the truth and leads you on the straight path to heaven."

"You mean a body can't git to heaven through no other church? You mean I can't make it?" exclaimed Hezzy.

"I don't like to say it so p'int blank as that. But I will say I favor my chances better'n yourn", declared Casty piously.

"Look here, I'm a deacon in my church, and Noah here is a elder in his. If folks like us can't git to heaven, who in hell can?" sputtered Hezzy angrily.

"Whoa! Right thar's a good place to stop", commanded Noah. "That's the trouble with these here arguments. Folks git all het up and git nowhars. Looks like the storm's done 'bout played out. It stirred up lots of wind and noise—jest like we been doing. It's turning off real nice out thar. You all can git home dry now and let me git back to work. So long Casty. Looks like the weather'll be good for tonight ...Bye, Will, remember me to your folks...Same to you Hezzy,"

"Benny, don't stand 'round looking at the sky. It ain't going to fall. Help Lay Fat load those sacks of fertilizer on his wagon.… I don't care if they do stink… You're in the feed business now, don't forgit. When you finish that, straighten up those sacks of laying mash what you throwed in the shed every which way. Then you can go home, and I'll close up the store. Git to it!"

Chapter 20

RAMBLING RECTORY

The pretentious rectory, by local standards, which housed the Episcopal clergy at Stanardsville, Virginia, never failed to make an indelible impression upon its successive occupants—not to say a scar. This structure in its special location had three eminent distinctions:

> It was the worst built house in the village and also the worst rectory north of the James River—or close to it.

> It was widely believed to be haunted.

> It enchanted those who lived a while under its roof who in later years remember more the pleasant moments than the days of stress.

THE WRECK

To take the first and very dubious distinction, suffice it to say that the dwelling was built of green lumber. All materials going into it were the cheapest possible, and the workmanship was unbelievably shoddy. At the time it was built, there did not seem to be anything resembling a building code in the whole county. If there had been, the structure would never have been approved by even the most incompetent inspector. Yet, for over half a century, it had housed more than half a dozen clerical families. During the same period, enough money was spent on it in repairs alone to have it torn down and rebuilt twice, even at modern inflated prices. It still stands upon its conspicuous knoll as pretentious as ever, far more comfortable for its dwellers, possessed of the same incomparable view of the mountains, shorn of church ownership, and with its demons banished.

Forty years ago, its state was far different. The weather boarding shrank with time, opening gaps that let in the wind unhindered, for there was no insulation, nor even building paper between the inside and outside walls. Beautiful wainscoting ornamented the interior of the downstairs rooms, but, with seasoning, the boards warped, opening large cracks so that not only could one see through them to the out-of-doors but strong winds blew dirt, sand and small gravel into the house. Thanks to the basic error of using green lumber at the start, the house creaked, groaned and moaned with each change of the temperature.

As a result the structure could be described as air-conditioned, delightfully cool in summer and terribly bitter in winter. So cold was it that when one used the telephone in the unheated front hall, it was necessary to put on a hat and overcoat, and in the worst weather—gloves. Our two little daughters, Margaret and Pattie, wore snow suits in the rambling house most of the cold season to keep reasonably warm in spite of the seven fires that had to be tended constantly, since most of them were wood fires. The only heat in the upstairs hallway came up through a grill in the floor above the coal stove in the dining room, just as the back upstairs bedroom was heated from the kitchen by keeping the door of the connecting stairway open all the time. Each bathroom was kept bearable by portable heaters. Even so it was comical to see the curtains wave and the toilet paper stand out almost straight in windy weather, though the windows were kept closed as tightly as possible. The space off the dining room, meant for storage, was the coldest spot of all, but it served us well as an unintentional ice box—or as my older daughter called it, "the fishrater room."

For a wonder, a better job was done on the plumbing, which gave no trouble except during thunderstorms. The electric line, which had been run in from the distant street, had not been properly grounded, and lightning produced weird and frightening effects. The electric lights during storms would dim and glow with an eerie color. Once a bluish fireball formed over the dining room table under the center light fixture. It was worse in the two bathrooms when electricity popped in the commodes and made black outlines of the stopper chains in the washbasins nearly every storm. When the trouble was finally diagnosed and corrected, life in the rectory lost much of its spice, but no one deplored the change.

All this was bad enough but there was the plastering! It must have been mixed to stay up on the ceilings and walls just long enough for the house to be paid for. A weaker, more lifeless, concoction, held up mainly by wall paper, can scarcely be imagined. Dangerous falls from the ceilings were frequent and repairs were made slowly because there were few plasterers that far out in the country. My wife and I lived in constant terror for the safety of our two baby daughters, continually testing the ceilings to find the safest places to put the cribs. Even then, we took the further precaution of putting lap boards or planks on top of the cribs at night for added protection. Falls were frequent, and at times they barely missed members of the family. Cleaning up after falls and subsequent repairs were a continual nuisance.

Gravity was not the only cause of these falls. Each year for three successive years, between Christmas and New Year's, mysterious fires broke out in the village after midnight, in every case destroying considerable business property. The last one swept away the bank, the feed store, the only restaurant, a filling station, a grocery, and the hardware store. But this was not all the damage.

I and my little family had slept through the beginning of the fire, quite unaware of what was happening, since the rectory was about a quarter of a mile from the center of the county seat. All of a sudden, there was a shattering sound and a shock, and the noise of breaking glass and falling plaster. Half awake, I found myself in the middle of the bedroom floor, conscious of a vast red light and a baby's crying. When I had gathered my wits, I went to the window, and it seemed that the whole town was ablaze. I made sure first that my family had suffered no harm. That done, I dressed hurriedly and went to find out what was happening.

On the way out, I discovered that the rectory had suffered considerable damage. The glass in seven windows on the village side of the rectory had been shattered. Plastering had fallen from portions of the ceiling in two rooms. In the downstairs living room almost all of the plastering of the southwest wall had collapsed, creating a choking cloud of dust, which settled over everything in the house. Since nothing seemed to require immediate attention around the home and because there were sounds of distress from where the fire was raging, I hurried over to see what had happened and whether or not I could render some help. However, by that time nothing could be done except to try to hold the conflagration within bounds until it died out, leaving as it did a scene of misery and desolation.

The explosion not only did much damage in the village, including blowing out windows and wrecking the Negro lodge hall, but broke many windows at a considerable distance from the settlement. It was remarkable that more harm had not been done. It was reported that several cases of dynamite had been stored in a small shack between the hardware store and the lodge hall, but on the store property. Not only were the cases piled up in the shelter, but inexplicably the boxes of dynamite caps were put on top of the dynamite. So when the hardware store caught fire, it was only a matter of minutes before the whole thing went up. Just in time, someone who knew of the danger shouted, "Run for your lives!" to the volunteer firefighters, who took shelter and so escaped injury. From that time on, there were no more such costly fires in Stanardsville. No one was legally accused of setting the fires but gossip was rampant for months. It was muttered by many, "I hope that whoever did it finally got the insurance he was after and will now let us live in peace!"

THE GHOSTS

Since the rectory was commonly regarded as a jinxed house, the legend of its being haunted seemed to grow naturally, even though its origin lay in certain prayer meetings, which were held for a time in the rectory. Someone gossiped that these were spiritualistic séances, which summoned ghosts to the building and from which they had never departed.

When my family and I took up residence in the rectory, it wasn't long before people in the village began asking veiled questions:

"How do you like living in the rectory?"

"Is everything all right over there?"

"Does anything bother you?"

"Have you seen or heard anything out of the way?"

We woke up finally to the fact that these were not just evidences of polite interest in our welfare. It became plain that many were convinced that the house was inhabited by spectral influences which to date had frightened a number of people but so far had harmed no one. Signs of such mysterious forces were numerous in the popular mind. Chief among them were these:

Cries and shrieks in the night, especially when the building was vacant.

Ghostly footfalls on the stairways.

Lights after dark with no known source passing from window to window upstairs.

Doors opened and closed with no one there.

Scratching within the walls.

Groans, screamings, and moans throughout the house, especially after midnight, when spirits are usually abroad.

Ghostly forms flitting around the rectory after dark.

Many of these signs were detected by people taking a shortcut without permission through the property in the evenings. This chatter about apparitions swelled the rumors. These intruders at night were not always on innocent errands and especially when court was in session. Toward the rear of the property, just back of the stable, there were four acres of young pines averaging seven feet in height and growing closely together. For some time it furnished admirable cover for moonshiners who brought down their wares from the mountains and dispensed them on church property. So heavy was the thicket that I was long unaware of the nature of so much coming and going in the back lot, thinking in innocence that they were just hill folk who, in their free and easy way, saw no harm in using the lot as a "nigh way" to town day and night.

The sheriff knew quite well what was going on and, in a puckish mood, would worry my church members by telling them now and then:

"The biggest bootleg operation around these parts is on your preacher's land. Maybe one of these days, I'll raid the place and put your preacher in jail. Won't that look good in the papers?"

Of course the raid never came. For one thing, the sheriff and I were good friends, but I shall never understand why he and my friends never told me about the illegal commerce about which I was too naive. However, one court day near Christmas, I and my older daughter, Margaret, hunted through the thicket looking for a suitable Christmas tree. We found a good tree, which pleased the little girl, but I also stumbled on a cache of moonshine put up in gallon jugs. From then on I was a wiser man. Immediately I requested Gene Toms, a neighbor who helped me take care of my place in return for using a portion of the land to raise corn for his horses, to get an assistant to destroy the whiskey and to cut down the growth of pines. This they did quickly and with such zest that I am suspicious to this day that they interpreted my orders broadly, but I saw no point in being too inquisitive. Anyway, most of the trespassing stopped and what remained was finished off when my dog loving wife, Constance, made herself a present of a Great Dane, whose size and voice commanded even my sincere respect.

Like all haunted houses, reason and research destroyed romance and put to flight every spook, making havoc of each manifestation of the spirit world. In most cases, the answers lay simply in the fact of green lumber and shoddy workmanship. When the lumber dried out thoroughly after construction, all portions of the building were somewhat out of kilter, and little of the framework fitted as it should have. No wonder doors opened and closed at every vibration and breeze when they hung so out of plumb. The ghostly foot-falls, especially at night, were only the contraction and expansion of warped floor boards at every change in temperature. Also they accounted for the groans, creakings, and "the things that go bump in the night."

The dim lights seen moving from window to window in the otherwise unlighted rectory after dark lost their mystic status with a little observation. Automobiles travelling on Route 33 from Gordonsville, going west, came into Stanardsville on a wide shallow curve. After sundown, along a short stretch, their headlights threw a ghostly illumination on the north and west second story windows and the glow moved from pane to pane as the cars traversed the section of the highway from which their light could strike the house.

The matter of pale, phantom forms flitting around the haunted house during the evening was rooted in the superstitious and frightened imaginations of trespassers on the property who started at every shadow and jumped at the rustle of every field mouse in the grass. Stray dogs accounted for many reported apparitions. But a sheep, which somehow got loose and wandered onto the property one night, terrified some late revelers who were short-cutting on the way home. Their frenzied and perfervid accounts of this ghost agitated the community for weeks and were added to the tales usually told about the house, which seemed to be lying under an evil curse.

However, the matter of the cries and shrieks, not to mention the scratchings within the walls, was not so easily disposed of, as I can testify from personal experience. Many times, I had heard the scratchings but put them down to the activities of rats, but I could never explain it to my satisfaction. Then came a night when I was alone in the rectory, painting woodwork in the front hall, trying to fill my loneliness with work, while my little family was spending some days with friends in Charlottesville.

It was about nine o clock and everything was still—eerily still—not a sound. All of a sudden from somewhere in the house, there was a loud scream, "Yeeeeow!", and then complete silence. My scalp prickled and my insides tied into a knot. If this wasn't an evil spirit, it was a reasonable facsimile thereof. It would do until the real thing came along. I put down my brush and studied the situation very carefully, assuring myself first that I had actually heard a scream. Convinced that it was not the result of my imagination, I knew that if I was to continue living in the building, I was compelled to find its source. Gathering my faculties and courage, I searched the building from top to bottom, not neglecting any corner or cranny, but to no avail. I found nothing and heard nothing further. That night I slept very little. The next day I continued the search but found no explanation of the chilling screech. For weeks afterward, worry gnawed at the back of my mind, but I did not mention the affair to anyone—not even to my wife.

One spring day, a year later, I stumbled fortunately on the solution of the hair raising mystery. At the time, I was putting in my garden and had occasion to go to the house to get a rake, which I kept with my other tools in the closet at the end of the back porch. As I approached the house, a yellow cat dashed across the yard and into the closet, whose door I had left open. As I was rather hostile to strange cats, I followed it into the closet in order to chase it off the premises. But once in the closet, whose only illumination was from the open door, I could find no trace of the feline. Thinking that it had hidden behind some of the clutter I kept in it, I got a flashlight and made a thorough search but without success.

As many times as I had been in the closet, I had only looked around but never up, because the upper part was always in darkness. I turned the beam of the flashlight toward the ceiling and found the clue to the solution of the mystery of the screams. The builder had skimped on materials here too. The weather boarding of the house wall did not go all the way to the ceiling of the closet. There was a gap of about ten inches and, since there was no insulation of any kind, this small opening gave any energetic cat easy access to the total space between all walls and between all floors of the house. This easily accounted for the weird scratchings heard when everything was quiet especially at night. The screech I heard doubtless occurred when some cat encountered a rat tougher than it was, for I had seen some large rodents at times about the place. I kept traps set but caught very few. I heard the scream on one or two other occasions and once, the odor, which developed subsequently, supported the belief that something—a cat or a rat—had come to a very bad end.

THE SPLENDOR AND THE MAGIC

Overbalancing all the deficiencies of this misbegotten rectory was the view of the Blue Ridge Mountains. Sitting in the swing on the front porch at the close of a clear spring day, one got a sense of ineffable peace and well-being, watching the interplay of colors on the tumbled mountains as the sun in the west slowly dropped from sight and its light died out. Covering the heights and valleys was a misty purple, which changed in intensity from place to place. As the sunset played on the upper slopes and shone through the passes, shades of color chased each other up and down the range almost in leapfrog style—golds, blues, oranges, violets—until they got lost in the deepening purple, fading to black as the stars came out, leaving only the dim outline of the upper reaches silhouetted against the night sky. Somehow, resting in the afterglow of such a spectacle, the worries of the day and the discomfort of living conditions lost their sting and, for the moment, seemed quite unimportant.

In the daytime, the hills frequently revealed a beauty of their own during the green months, and even in the harsh winters they had their passing phases of splendor. The blue color was almost always present, veiling the mountains. Yet there was no sameness since the changes of mood of both the observer and of nature altered the prospect from moment to moment.

The nearer scenes cast their spell also. When the eye dropped from the mountains, it fell on a delightful small meadow, extending from the highway toward the rectory. It was relaxingly green for three seasons out of four, except in periods of extreme drought. Next, on the fore slope of the rectory knoll, were several apple trees, which contributed their springtime glory. Where the yard met the edge of the orchard, we grew flowers. They reached the pinnacle of beauty the year we planted a long ten foot wide strip of cosmos across the width of the property, which not only gave us pleasure but also the people of the village who could see it plainly from the business section.

Crowning the hill around the house were several giant oak trees, which in summer were generous with heavy shade in hot weather. The constant breezes made it a welcome place to sit when the pressure of work eased off. The memory of a father still sees two little girls, now mothers, playing and laughing happily under the trees. Now and then, his mood is akin to that of the German poet Eichendorf:

O hatt' ich, hatt' ich Flugel,
Zu fliegen da hinein-

(O would that I, would that I had wings,
To fly away there!)

181

Back of the rectory was ample space for our feathered flocks—pigeons, chickens, ducks, and geese. Going down grade past a beautiful crabapple tree, which furnished delicious jelly, one came on our wonderful garden, lying on a southern slope, generous with food and flowers. Five sections of land were separated by drainage ditches that served to carry off rain water and the wash from drenching thunderstorms. Each section, or plot, was bordered by plants of one kind of flower. This one sported chrysanthemums; that one zinnias; another dahlias; its neighbor marigolds, and the fifth gaillardias. Different vegetables filled the center portion of each section—cauliflower, bush beans, snaps, cabbages, beets and carrots. On the semi-circular hillside, Irish potatoes, sweet corn and tomatoes throve and produced bountifully. The whole presented a pleasing sight, creating a spell of plenty and of peace.

With the passing years, it is strange how under the magic wand of memory, the sad and the ugly are filtered out, and both house and hill become an enchanted spot where one is glad to have spent a while.